PRAISE FOR *NOT ON MY WATCH*

"*Not on My Watch* captures the passion and calling of Elizabeth Johnston and everyone who values faith, family, and freedom. This spunky mother of ten homeschooled children and a faithful wife to an equally busy husband has every excuse to watch the culture wars from the sidelines. Propelled into Christian activism by the story of Kentucky Clerk Kim Davis in 2015, Elizabeth set ablaze social media and soon became rightly known as the Activist Mommy. Her personal story is inspiring. This book is well-written and will inspire you. *Not on My Watch* is a must-read."

Mathew D. Staver, Esq., B.C.S.

Founder and chairman, Liberty Counsel

"*Not on My Watch* will inspire mama bears across the world and teach them how to fight for their children."

Sam Sorbo

Filmmaker, actress, author, and homeschool advocate

"What a blessing it has been to know Elizabeth Johnston and her amazing family for so many years! Their love for God and people is a powerful testimony of God's grace in their lives, and Elizabeth's uncompromising commitment to speak truth and stand for righteousness both inside and outside her home has elevated her to prominence at a time when our nation needs 'mama bears' the most! We thank God for her voice and highly recommend you read and apply the truths from *Not on My Watch*."

David and Jason Benham

Nationally acclaimed entrepreneurs, speakers, and best-selling authors

"As the events of 2015 surrounding same-sex marriage and religious freedom exploded, I was faced with an opposition of the most fierce kind. So when Elizabeth Johnston and her family rolled onto the scene in Morehead, Kentucky, she saw and experienced a culture war that inspired her to speak up and become known as the Activist Mommy. She has become a passionate and tireless voice and is an inspiration for all of us. It is not a matter of *if* our Christian values will be challenged; it is only a matter of *when* we will face opposition. Elizabeth is sounding the call to action. For this busy mother, silence is not an option. Elizabeth is not afraid to declare truth and to declare it boldly in her new book, *Not on My Watch*. May the title of this book describe all who call upon the name of the Lord."

Kim Davis

Former Rowan County (Kentucky) Clerk

and author of *Under God's Authority*

"When the Lord inaugurated the New Covenant, He used an unlikely source to pave the way. John the Baptist rightly belonged in the Jewish temple serving as a priest. Yet he was called to be Christ's forerunner. God has raised in our day an unlikely source to call America to her senses; to fight against the regressive efforts to move our nation further away from God and toward secular humanism, sexual deviancy, and the slavery of Marxism. Elizabeth Johnston, a wife and home-school mother of ten children, has sounded the alarm: NOT ON MY WATCH! May the nation echo this call and join this cause!"

Abraham Hamilton III

General counsel and public policy analyst,

American Family Association

"What accounts for the sensation of the Activist Mommy? It is merely a mama bear, Elizabeth Johnston, being faithful over many years as a wife, mother, and committed Christian. Her private life produced the fruit of her public life. This book is a merger of both. I highly recommend it."

Rev. Rusty Lee Thomas

National director, Operation Save America

"Elizabeth Johnston's commitment to the Word of God is a delight to experience in all she does. *Not on My Watch* is a personification of this commitment and an inspiration to those who might be standing on the sidelines wondering what to do next in this war on Christians and our families. I felt a sense of hope as I read this book—a must-read for all Christians, but especially moms!"

Molly Smith

President, Cleveland Right to Life

"This is war. Never in the history of the United States have our freedoms, faith, families, and children in the womb been under such relentless attack as right now. Making matters worse, our religious and political leaders surrender our constitutional rights and protections by failing to recognize the Marxist strategies and tactics of the Left. With both wit and wisdom, the Activist Mommy shows us how to oppose the ideologies that threaten the foundations of our constitutional republic. Not everybody can be the Activist Mommy, but we can all join the fight and actively protect our faith, families, and children in the womb."

Patrick Martin

Outreach and development director, Alaska Right to Life

"*Not on My Watch* is a must-read for every mom concerned for the future of our children, our country, and our out-of-control culture. A refreshing perspective from a mom turned activist, Elizabeth Johnston brings much needed 'mommy sense' to a world saturated with nonsense."

Kimberly Fletcher

President and founder, Moms for America, Inc.

"We are living in frightening times—but Elizabeth Johnston isn't letting fear keep her off the battlefield. Her courage and straight talk is inspiring a generation of mothers to stand in the gap for their children. If you're struggling to find your voice or if you wonder if this battle really can be won, be encouraged! *Not on My Watch* is a guidebook for parents who no longer wish to be sidelined by a politically correct culture. As a mother of seven, I applaud Elizabeth for leading the way back toward truth in a culture that is in desperate need of it. *Not on My Watch* is a must-read for every parent and grandparent who wants to make a positive difference in the lives of the next generation."

Heidi St. John aka The Busy Mom

Mother of seven, podcaster, speaker, and author of *Becoming MomStrong*

"From the moment I began to read this adventure of North America's warrior princess against all things evil and ridiculous, my heart started to beat faster, and it never stopped. Every word, every story, every triumph, every truth that is offered to help us stand with courage breathed life into my soul and ignited something deep within me. Reading *Not on My Watch* evoked tears, anger, and laughter, and it caused my being to bow in surrender asking for help from heaven as we wrestle on earth with the evil that Elizabeth exposes time after time. Activist Mommy is my hero, and she is fearless like a hurricane. Read *Not on My Watch* and feel the wind of God's Spirit calling you into the battle."

Laura-Lynn Tyler Thompson

Canadian activist and author of *Relentless Redemption*

"If you're looking for Elizabeth Johnston, you'll find her leading a heroic effort on the front lines of wherever the battle is the hottest. I recommend her book because I have seen her in action. She's the real deal, and her godly children are a testimony that you can be a successful mom *and* an activist!"

Janet Porter

Author and president of Faith2Action

NOT ON MY WATCH

NOT ON MY WATCH

How to win the fight for family, faith, and freedom

Elizabeth Johnston

THE ACTIVIST MOMMY

WORTHY®
PUBLISHING
New York • Nashville

Worthy
Hachette Book Group
1290 Avenue of the Americas, New York, NY 10104
worthypublishing.com
twitter.com/worthypub

First Edition: February 2019

Worthy is a division of Hachette Book Group, Inc. The Worthy name and logo are trademarks of Hachette Book Group, Inc.

The publisher is not responsible for websites (or their content) that are not owned by the publisher.

Author photos: Kathleen Dellinger | Captured by KD Photography
Cover design concept: Flood Creative Agency (floodcreative.co)
Cover and interior design: Bart Dawson

Library of Congress Cataloging-in-Publication Data
Names: Johnston, Elizabeth, (Conservative activist blogger) author.
Title: Not on my watch : how to win the fight for family, faith, and freedom / Elizabeth Johnston, the Activist Mommy.
Description: New York: Worthy, an imprint of Hachette Book Group [2019]
Identifiers: LCCN 2018033741 | ISBN 9781683972617 (hardcover)
Subjects: LCSH: Christians--Political activity--United States. | Christianity and politics--United States--History--20th century. | Christianity and culture--United States.
Classification: LCC BR516 .J64 2019 | DDC 261.0973--dc23
LC record available at https://lccn.loc.gov/2018033741

ISBN: 978-1-68397-261-7 (hardcover), 978-1-68397-217-4 (ebook), 9781545910757 (audio book)

Printed in the United States of America

LSC-C

10 9 8 7 6 5 4 3 2 1

To my ten amazing children, whose liberty is the reason I fight. Your innocence is my preoccupation and your future children's liberty is my obsession. There would be no Activist Mommy and no *Not on My Watch* without you. I love all ten of you with my whole heart and thank you so much for all you've done and sacrificed to help your mommy fight for truth, freedom, and righteousness. Hopefully, you will have a much brighter future because of the work we as a family have done to push back the darkness.

To my mom and dad, for teaching me how to fight and persevere against all odds. I love you both!

To my pastor, Ante, who called out the "Deborah" in me in 2015. You saw in me something I was afraid to see: that God was about to rocket me out of my comfort zone for such a time as this. Some men are too prideful or intimidated to recognize a call on a woman's life, but not you. Thank you so much for believing in me.

To my husband, my biggest cheerleader and helper in this life. Your constant encouragement and vision for greater accomplishments has helped me reach heights I never dreamed possible. Fear of failure would have snuffed out my work many times, but alas, I'm married to the consummate visionary, and you are always there rooting me on to take bigger risks. I thank you for that and love you so much. Thank you for the hours you put into this project. It would never have happened without you. We have made some waves and done some crazy things. There is no one I'd rather do crazy stuff with more than you.

NOT ON MY WATCH

CONTENTS

FOREWORD
BY TODD STARNES

In this world there are mama bears who will do anything to protect their children. And then there's Elizabeth Johnston—she's a mama grizzly.

I first met Elizabeth several years ago when she faced the wrath of the nameless, faceless censors at Facebook. After sharing her story with the nation, the social media giant temporarily backed off. But since then she has faced an onslaught of cyberspace bullies in her noble quest to protect not just her children, but every child in the nation. The attacks have been vicious, but Elizabeth never backed down. She stood her ground and quickly became known as the Activist Mommy.

It's amazing how God uses the most unsuspecting people to advance the Kingdom work—from Moses to David to the apostle Paul. So maybe it should not be that surprising that the Lord decided to choose a mother of ten from North Carolina to become a mighty culture warrior.

She single-handedly exposed the radical sex agenda at *Teen Vogue* and launched the global Sex Ed Sit Out movement. Her bold stand earned her accolades from many Christian leaders, including Franklin Graham. That's why I'm so excited for you to read *Not on My Watch: How to Win the Fight for Family, Faith, and Freedom*."

This book will equip moms and dads with the essential tools they need to fight the good fight in our rapidly changing culture. Elizabeth does not shy away from the controversial and downright politically incorrect topics of the day—from natural marriage to abortion to the war on gender to the sexualization of children.

I want you to read this book, devour every sentence, and then share it with your friends and family members and church members. This is the kind of book that can rock the culture to its very foundation. And don't be surprised by the time you read the last page that you, too, have become a mama or papa grizzly.

Todd Starnes
Fox News Channel

INTRODUCTION

*The Left has been advancing and claiming more
and more territory while we have attended church
and been content to wait for Jesus to come back.*

'm a simple homeschooling mom who lives on a small farm with my hubby, ten kids, horses, chickens, cats, and a dog. For a year, I have used Scotch tape to rig my phone to the rearview mirror of my fifteen-passenger van (or bus, as people like to call it) while I rant about the social and moral issues that cause me as a mom and a conservative Christian grave concern. One thing has become clear since I began this journey as the Activist Mommy—God uses simple, willing vessels who can't be bullied or bribed.

At times Facebook and Twitter have suspended my accounts, YouTube and Google have denied monetization of my pages, and numerous media outlets have written outrageous hit pieces about me and my family. Stories about the Left's censorship of me have hit *Fox and Friends*, the *New York Times,* and beyond.

Why me? Well, to the CEOs at Google, Twitter, and Facebook, I'm a social and political heretic. And, even worse, I've shown them that they don't intimidate me. I've learned how to run headfirst into difficult situations and trust God for the outcome. I've learned how to embrace controversy and use it to expose the intolerance, hypocrisy, and immorality of the Left. I've learned to laugh at their bigotry. (They haaaaaate being laughed at more than anything!) I've learned that personal opposition and character assassinations are simply stepping-stones to increase your reach and influence, if you will only stay the course and remain humble. Because I've learned to do the above, I am hated by the Left and celebrated by everyday citizens who don't have a large platform to spread their ideas.

In only one year, my following on Facebook organically grew from seven thousand to half a million. Yes, all while scotch-taping my phone to the rearview mirror of my van, breastfeeding my babies, changing diapers, homeschooling ten kids, burning *Teen Vogue* magazines, launching a global movement to fight graphic sex ed, and shutting down sex-trafficking brothels. Quite an odd spread of activity there, wouldn't you say? Desperate times deserve desperate measures.

It should be obvious that the world around us has gone stark raving mad. Right is wrong and wrong is right. Men are now allowed to be in girls' locker rooms and restrooms and vice versa. Three thousand babies are killed every day in America through abortion,[1] and our tax dollars are paying for Planned Parenthood execs to get rich off the blood money of those innocent babies. Drag queens who identify as alien killer clowns are reading books about gender identity to preschoolers during story hour in tax-subsidized libraries.[2] Children in public schools are being taught Islamic prayers from the "peaceful" Muslim religion,[3] but the Christian God and Christian holidays are deemed dangerous by many and are banned from the public schools. Yes, you heard that right. Muhammad is now peaceful and Jesus is dangerous. Somebody get me some duct tape before my head explodes!

Let's get one thing straight: the reason we are in this mess is because Christians lack courage and have weak stomachs for controversy and confrontation. Granted, I've pretty much always been the kind of person who bucks the status quo, fights for the under-dog, and pokes the tyrannical bear with a stick. You might say my personality is kind of built for battle. But I receive frequent messages from people who are gripped by fear that prevents them from speaking up at their jobs, their schools, their city council meetings, and even in the presence of their own family members.

Why are we so fearful, when we have *no* shortage in God's Word of examples of courageous believers? Our heritage is chock-full of Christian heroes! Noah was likely ridiculed for 150 years as he obeyed God and built the ark. Shadrach, Meshach, and Abed-Nego courageously defied their tyrannical king and were willing to be burned alive in order to remain faithful to their God. Daniel prayed with the windows wide open, publicly defying the king's orders. It was as if Daniel was mocking the leaders with "Nah-nee-nah-nee-boo-boo! Come arrest me!" God defended him and promoted him for his public courage and resistance to an ungodly law. The Hebrew midwives defied orders and saved the little Jewish babies, risking their lives by disobeying Pharaoh's decree. The apostles turned the world upside down and preached boldly when the authorities forbade them.[4] These heroic individuals from God's Word are more than ample examples to imitate, but few are doing so, and now we risk the threat of losing our freedoms.

In a culture that's trying to silence Christians, how should we respond? How did Jesus respond when His enemies tried to silence Him and Pilate threatened to kill Him? Did He say, "Okay, I won't rock the boat" or "I'll go along to get along, lest I offend someone"? No, He said, "You could have no power at all against Me unless it had been given you from above" (John 19:11). We should respond with that same courage and confidence. We are the salt and light of the world! And the Bible says if we lose our saltiness we are good for nothing except to be trodden underfoot by men! (Matthew 5:13–14).

I believe we have a dearth in our nation of bold, unwavering Christians who are willing to address and take action on the burning social issues of the day that are destroying our souls, our families, and our country. I also believe God's Word has the answer to all of these issues. So I began the Activist Mommy with the desire to apply what God's Word says to the untouchable, politically incorrect issues of abortion, Islam, radical feminism, homosexuality, and the attack on the natural family.

Just look at some of the stories in the headlines these days:

- Not only are homosexuals forcing bakers to bake their same-sex-wedding cakes; now Satanists are attempting to force Christian bakers to bake their satanic cakes.[5]
- Schools with uniform requirements are changing to gender-free clothing so no one gets offended.[6]
- Another football coach was fired for praying with his students.[7]
- The Boston City Hall plaza will fly the gay pride flag, transgender flag, and flags of communist countries, but won't fly the Christian flag![8]
- Planned Parenthood was actually in the running for the Nobel Peace Prize Award.[9] (Yes, you read that correctly!)

- Middle school students are being taught, at taxpayer expense, pornographic, gender-bending, sex education in public schools.

This is war! And if you're waiting around for a quick little rapture fix to get you out of this mess, you are not a soldier in this battle. Pastor Wade Trimmer said this about the modern Christian church: "We're the only team I've ever played on that preaches a victorious Christ and roots for the opposition (the anti-Christ) to win so that we can get off the field! After all, 'The quicker they fry, the quicker we fly!'"[10] Pssssh! He's right. Think about it. For the last fifty years, the church has been throwing Super Bowl parties and playing Twister in youth group, while the Left has taken crucial battlefield after battlefield. Abortion. Same-sex marriage. Pornography. Education. Removing God from the public square. The Left has been advancing and claiming more and more territory while we have attended church and been content to wait for Jesus to come back. This is not the attitude or teaching of Scripture. Jesus said, "Occupy till I come" (Luke 19:13 KJV). He didn't say, "Hide till I come" or "Hunker down till I come."

What are you doing to occupy and build His kingdom till He returns? What would happen to our world if the eighty million evangelicals who are praying, "Come quickly, Lord Jesus" were at the abortion factories every day, praying and witnessing? I'll tell you. Abortion would end. What if the eighty million evangelicals said we would boycott the internet until pornography is banned and obscenity laws are enforced? I guarantee you in a skinny minute, internet porn would be dealt a huge blow. Eighty million customers are a lot of customers! But we're too busy entertaining ourselves on our phones and watching television to build God's kingdom on the earth. We're too busy arguing about whether we're Calvinists or Armenians to unite and change things.

Have you ever noticed how soldiers on the front lines of a battle don't have time for petty squabbles? They're too busy rescuing the perishing for pettiness. If you've got time for pettiness, you need to enlist in the army. You need to get on the front lines. Before long you'll have so many darts and bullets coming at you and bouncing off of you by God's Spirit that you will care less about doctrinal divisions and petty differences.

We must unite if we want to win this war for our children, our morals, our freedom, and our culture. Do you want your kids to grow up in an America where the Bible is hate speech and you're thrown in jail for preaching it? Canadians are already being placed in jail for preaching what the Bible says on homosexuality.[11] If you just lie down and take it, what's next? Do you want your kids to grow up in an America where our country's leaders are open Muslims and where speaking against Islam is a hate crime? Our country is being transformed before our eyes by godless, Marxist social engineers whose idols are Alfred Kinsey, Barack Obama, and Saul Alinksy. Will you sit silent and let them succeed?

No! Not on my watch! My children and grandchildren will know I worked tirelessly to proclaim the gospel, push back the darkness, and keep our country free. Social Marxists are praying (hexing, voodooing, séancing, or whatever they do) that you don't read this book, because it is a threat to their comfortable existence. In *Not on My Watch*, I will show you how to win against the Left's attack on free speech, the Left's obsession with the sexualization of children, and the Left's attack on natural marriage.

I'm sick of losing to the Left. I'm grieved watching my country's morality and founding principles get flushed down the toilet of political correctness and perversion. I'm done with sucking my thumb after the social Marxists win another Twitter boycott campaign or another million vagina hatters show up for a protest march. I am one simple mom who has gotten off the sidelines and seen some pretty incredible victories in two short, action-packed years. If God can use me to expose *Teen Vogue*, shut down sex brothels, and launch a global movement to end graphic, gender-bending sex ed, what could He do through each of us if we all engaged in the fight for life, liberty, and righteousness? With God all things are possible.

Who is ready to start winning?

CHAPTER 1

OUT OF YOUR DENS, MAMA BEARS!

*Nothing frustrates me more than hearing
Christians say, "We are supposed to just preach
the gospel, not fight a culture war."
Grr! No, actually, no.*

t was a day I will always remember. As the mother of nine home-schooled kids and six months pregnant with my tenth, I was facing laundry piled up as tall as my five-foot-three frame, stacks of papers to grade, two sinks full of dishes, and more bills piled on my desk than there was money in our always slender bank account. But something burned inside me I couldn't ignore as I read the news that day.

I could identify with and understand the small, bold woman I watched on my computer screen, who was at that moment the talk of the nation.

I had been loosely following an unfolding conflict in Kentucky as Kim Davis, a county clerk, refused to sign a same-sex marriage license because of her biblical convictions. Her life was being dissected by every news organization in the nation. The sins of her past were being broadcast to the whole world. There was no sincere attempt by the media to understand her motive for not wanting to endorse same-sex marriage. She was ruthlessly mocked by the LGBT community. She was targeted with vulgar death threats,[1] and even her church received bomb threats. Her friends and family, the ones she loved the most, were now in danger because of her principled stance. She had every reason to just throw in the towel and sign on the dotted rainbow line.

The same-sex couples who were walking into Kim's office for a license could easily go to the neighboring county clerk for their marriage licenses, but they were activists and were targeting Kim, who refused to be bullied or bribed or threatened into bowing to their god of political correctness. They would not rest until every single Christian county clerk in America was bullied into defiling their conscience and signing same-sex marriage licenses.

I walked over to the refrigerator and got my toddler a sippy cup and changed the baby's diaper. I sat back down before my laptop and clicked on a video being broadcast from a Kentucky news station. Kim Davis was behind the counter in her office, completely swarmed by cameras and reporters as two men angrily yelled at her and reporters bombarded her with questions. I was struck by how calm and soft-spoken, yet firm, she was while responding to these outsiders. When Kim told the same-sex couple she would not be issuing marriage licenses that day, the tension grew and the homosexual couple was indignant.

"Under whose authority are you refusing to issue us a marriage license?" the homosexual asked as the television cameras zoomed in.

Without missing a beat, Davis responded, "Under God's authority."[2]

That's it! Those were the words I had been waiting to hear. I immediately said to my children, "Kids, pack your bags. We're going to Kentucky." I wasn't about to let my children miss this opportunity to watch up close this bold woman of God take a stand for God and His Word.

Kim Davis knew what she had said was politically incorrect and that the nation would be watching. She didn't care. She knew she had just infuriated the Left and would be ruthlessly targeted. She didn't care. Her devotion for God outweighed the opinions of people. I decided nothing was stopping me from having my children participate in this heroic show down of faith.

"Under God's authority." That's how God dynamited me out of my chair in my homeschool room in Ohio and onto the front lines of the culture war.

RALLYING THE TROOPS

Never had I so clearly visualized the clear and present threat to my children and their future liberty, and I was prepared to do whatever little ol' me could do to remove that threat.

I got on Facebook immediately and began to rally my friends. Thirty-five of us from several different states hastily packed and drove to Kentucky to arrive in time for the morning trial. We found hundreds of people standing outside the courthouse rallying around Kim and traditional marriage, as well as about forty people who came hoping to see a victory for the LGBT community. The sun beat down on us as we prayed and sang outside the courthouse, asking God to vindicate Kim and protect the religious liberty of Christians in America.

At the trial, the worst we expected was that Kim Davis would be demoted or lose her job. The thought of that infuriated us. Never in a million years did we suspect what was about to happen. Judge David Bunning decided to make a national statement and placed

Kim in wrist and ankle shackles and threw her in jail, telling her she wasn't getting out until she was willing to sign same-sex marriage licenses! I could not believe how far gone we were that we would let this federal judge overrule the will of the people of Kentucky and persecute this Christian clerk who was simply following Kentucky law and her religion.

I wanted to encourage Kim Davis so badly, so we went with our nine kids in tow and one in the belly ready to visit every local jail facility till we found her.

At our second stop, a van swiftly pulled up to the jail, and inside of it we saw a handcuffed Kim. "We love you, Kim! We're praying for you, Kim! You're not alone! You're a hero!"

A Christian went to jail that day in America for simply acting like a Christian. I was shocked! How did we get here?

My husband had to go back to work in Ohio. As a physician, he had patients scheduled on Monday. I implored him, "Let us stay, honey. We can't leave yet. Kim is in jail. There is still work to do here." I knew I was pushing him out of his comfort zone. He is a family man and hates coming home to an empty house at the end of a hard day of work. But he saw the fire in my eyes, and he fanned it and let us stay.

The national media followed us everywhere. We sat down for continental breakfast beside CNN and MSNBC reporters. We bumped into New York media moguls in the elevator. Our small band of a few dozen believers gave them something to report as we fired up our campaign to get Kim out of jail. We were the boots on the ground. We created flyers and banners and networked with pastors, organized a rally, and handed out leaflets at their ball games. We flew speakers in from around the country. We worked hard to keep the story alive, while encouraging God's people to rally around Kim and demanding the leftist judge to free Kim Davis.

Over 75 percent of Kentuckians had overwhelmingly voted against same-sex marriage. Federal courts cannot make laws, according to the U.S. Constitution, much less make laws that over-rule the state constitutions. Kim Davis was obeying the law. Our rallying cry became, "Show us the law, or free Kim Davis!"

The most controversial thing we did was protest outside Judge Bunning's house. And it worked! After days of protesting and hold-ing a huge rally at the jail with ten thousand people in attendance, baking on the asphalt of the jail parking lot in blistering heat, we watched with amazement as Kim Davis walked out of that jail with a wide smile on her face and her hands uplifted in praise!

It was three of the most memorable and exciting weeks of my kids' lives. They still recall that time in Kentucky with tremendous fondness. They will never forget what God did and how He used our feeble efforts to get our dear sister out of jail.

THE GOVERNMENT IS NOT GOD

We urged Kentucky governor Steve Beshear and the Kentucky legislature to uphold God's law and Kentucky law and resist the unlawful decision from the federal judiciary. Beshear did not, and as a result, the election soon after the Kim Davis fiasco saw the executive branch in Kentucky go from Democrat to Republican for the first time in almost four decades with the election of Matt

Bevin, because Bevin was a very vocal supporter of Kim Davis and religious liberty.

Kim Davis had Kentucky law and the people of Kentucky on her side. Since 2004, the Kentucky Constitution had read, "Only a marriage between one man and one woman shall be valid or recognized as a marriage in Kentucky. A legal status identical or substantially similar to that of marriage for unmarried individuals shall not be valid or recognized."[3] Not only were they defining marriage between a man and a woman, but they weren't compromising to accept same-sex "civil unions."

When the Supreme Court ruled that states must accept same-sex marriage, they usurped their lawful boundaries. The United States Constitution tells us who has the power to create law, and it's not the judiciary: "All legislative Powers herein granted shall be vested in a Congress of the United States" (article 1, section 1).

If "all" lawmaking power is vested in Congress, is there any left for the courts? No. Kim Davis didn't violate any law; therefore her incarceration was lawless. It was kidnapping, according to the laws of the land. Wrong doesn't suddenly become right because a guy in a black robe violates the law to kidnap an innocent person and put her in a cage. I mean, can a judge rape someone and it be okay because he's a judge? What if he does it in a judge's attire in a courtroom, with a gavel in his hand? No, of course not! He's not the standard of right and wrong. Our rights come from God, not man. They're inalienable, which means they cannot be legitimately infringed upon except for punishment for a crime. Might does not make right. Just because Judge Bunning and his gun-totin' accomplices can shackle and cage an innocent person in violation of the law and the state and federal constitutions, that doesn't mean it's okay. He's the criminal!

The ninth and tenth amendments to the U.S. Constitution limit the federal government to specifically enumerated powers, and any right or duty not given to the feds belongs to the states or the people. The feds are oath-bound to obey the Constitution, which gives them their power in the first place. If the Constitution may be trampled, then upon what basis must we obey a thing they say?

The federal government isn't the master of the states. It is the servant of the states, with limited jurisdiction. They can only do what the contract says they can do, and even if something needs to be done that's not being done, they can't do it without an amendment authorizing them to do it. You don't amend the Constitution by violating it.

"JUST PREACH THE GOSPEL"

Nothing frustrates me more than hearing Christians say, "We are supposed to just preach the gospel, not fight a culture war." Grr! No, actually, no. In the Great Commission, Jesus told His disciples to teach the nations "all things that I have commanded you" (Matthew 28:20). How many things? *All* things! Man shall not live by bread alone, but by what, according to Jesus? "By every word that proceeds from the mouth God" (4:4). To abandon any word of God for fear of man or want of man's approval is to abandon faithfulness to God's Word, "for whoever shall keep the whole law, and yet stumble in one point, he is guilty of all" (James 2:10).

We have so much opportunity and freedom in America, and yet in one generation, a snoozing church has seen almost sixty million babies dismembered and slain by abortion and funded at taxpayers' expense,[4] the institution of marriage trampled by homosexuals, Ten Commandment monuments ripped out of our courthouse grounds and off our public school property by the atheists, and "safe sex" education programs teaching sodomy, premarital sex, oral sex, and mutual masturbation to our children by Planned Parenthood, again at taxpayers' expense. We have squandered our opportunities, which were even more expansive than what the first disciples had in the book of Acts!

Apathetic believers, reclined on their couches with their remote-controlled entertainment, their fishing boats, and their cell phone smut, are passing to our children and grandchildren a culture in which the Bible will be hate speech. We can't appeal to the Great Commission to justify our apathy. Yes, we should preach the gospel and tell people that Jesus is certainly coming back, but generations of Christians have been saying that while doing nothing to preserve religious freedom for their posterity. The Great Commission and soon-coming Savior should be a motivation to stand—not to cower, hide, and give up.

I FOUND MY VOICE

When Kim Davis walked out of jail that day and pointed heavenward, thanking God, tears filled my eyes! She was just an ordinary woman who had an extraordinary opportunity to stand in the face of tyranny and do right, and she chose to glorify God in her suffering. The day Kim was released from jail was a Wednesday, which is typically when churches have their midweek services. I discovered where she attended church and called to be sure they were meeting. Remember, although my children and I had been beating the streets for Kim, we had still never met her. As we pulled our big family van up to the church parking lot, we were greeted by a tall man who was clearly guarding the church and watching for potential threats. It was Kim's husband, Joe. Worshiping with Kim, and watching her praise the Lord in her little country church the first night she was out of jail, thrilled my soul!

While the church of Jesus Christ slumbers comfortably in their padded church pews, Kim Davis went to bat for all of us by challenging the seats of political power, going to jail for her faith, and ultimately planting a stake in the ground for religious freedom. My children and I will always admire her. In Kim Davis, a humble county clerk and relatively new convert to Christianity, I found a hero. I found courage outside my comfort zone. I found my voice. And I witnessed how God can use simple people like you and me to change the course of history, if we will only live our lives under God's authority.

--- **CHAPTER 2** ---

GENDER INSANITY

Since we didn't crush this PC stupidity fast enough,
things have gone from bad to worse.

When same-sex marriage was *legalized* nationally in June 2015 through *Obergefell v. Hodges*, Christians and natural family advocates warned that it would open a Pandora's box of perversion and confusion that would be virtually impossible to close. We were mocked and called doomsayers and bigots. But we learned all too quickly that we were right. It serves as a good reminder that when we abandon God's principles, we abandon reason and wisdom. When we allowed same-sex marriage as a culture, we opened ourselves up to a flood of sexual anarchy. It's as if the dam of protection and restraint was breached, and now we are drowning in perversion and confusion.

TARGET ANNOUNCES A NEW POLICY

When Target, the second-largest general merchandise retailer in America, announced they were changing their bathroom policy to accommodate whatever gender a person identified as (as opposed to their biological gender), most of middle America was in total shock! For the vast majority of us, this had never been an issue, and we found it hard to wrap our minds around why any company would legitimize such psychotic behavior as pretending to be someone of the opposite sex.

Many of us small business owners found it especially hard to believe that a company would choose to offend a majority of its customers for the sake of less than 1 percent of the population. I think we thought to ourselves, *Oh, we can fix this. We will show up in droves to protest Target, and they will protect their shareholders and bottom line by reversing their policy.* But we underestimated how stubborn and persistent social Marxists will be, even to their own detriment.

TARGET PROTEST

Several of my activist friends and ministry leaders scheduled a phone call about this new deluge of bathroom insanity. We all agreed this situation with Target was only the beginning and would soon be rolled out nationwide with the ultimate goal of forcing even our churches to allow the opposite sex in bathrooms. We determined that we had better hit this dangerous policy hard right from the outset, if we were going to maintain religious liberty.

Our friend Coach Dave Daubenmire was on that phone call and made media headlines by standing outside a Target bathroom with a sign that read, "Danger! Men May Be in Women's Restroom!" while his daughter used the Target bathroom.[1] That video went viral, and the American Family Association (AFA) used one of Coach's videos, in which he speaks to Target management to confirm the company's policy, to promote their Boycott Target petition drive.[2] The AFA petition was signed by one and a half million people who were fed up with the social Marxists' attack on the family,[3] and they pledged to never shop at Target unless the company reversed its new bathroom policy.

Protests began to pop up at Target stores all over the nation.

Not many things ignite conservatives to get out and hold a sign and protest, but this did. Locally, we had about fifty show up at our small-town Target to let our voices be heard and to field media interviews.

Coach Dave asked me to consider filming a video on this issue to call the mama bears to action and give the Target boycott a boost. I wasn't sure it would do much good or that many people would watch it. Who would care what a homeschool mom with ten children had to say?

This was actually the official beginning of the Activist Mommy. It took me forever to make that first video. I had to film it over and over to get it right. Eventually I eked out something that resonated with mama bears around the nation. I asked America, "How is it that 0.1 percent of the population have 99 percent of the population scrambling to accommodate their feelings?" The damage done to Target was immediate! America said enough is enough, and we voted with our pocketbooks. Target has since lost $15 billion, persisting in their stubbornness. They eventually ate crow and admitted that their handling of the transgender bathroom policy was what caused their sudden financial trouble.[4]

OBAMA'S BATHROOM DIRECTIVE

Then there was Obama's bathroom directive, and—holy guacamole!—did things ever get insane!

The crazy libs on the Charlotte (NC) City Council had approved an ordinance that would bring crazy town to not just federal government buildings but right to the public schools as well. As if children don't have enough to worry about in school with peer pressure, grades, drugs, social media, and navigating the ever-complicated world of relationships, they were now going to have to figure out gym class with a boy in the girls' locker room. Lord, have mercy! So the good ol' Southern gentlemen and gentlewomen of the North Carolina legislature quickly called a special session and passed a "bathroom bill" called HB2 to ensure that bathrooms/locker rooms/dressing rooms would be used only by individuals according to their biological sex at birth.

Whew! North Carolina legislators had put the Charlotte City Council in its place. Wait . . . not so fast! The Left never misses an opportunity for chaos. So radical-communist-Saul-Alinsky-worshiping Barack Hussein Obama sicced the Department of Justice on North Carolina and threatened to pull funding from the state if legislators did not obey His Majesty's Royal Bathroom Edict and let boys pee in the girls' room and vice versa. He wasn't about to let those redneck-Bible-totin', flag-waving North Carolinians defend their children with chivalrous manhood.

The Obama bathroom letter, dated May 13, 2016, which was sent to schools nationwide by the Departments of Justice and Education, stated, "A school may not require transgender students to use facilities inconsistent with their gender identity or to use individual-user facilities when other students are not required to do so."[5] The edict implicitly threatened that schools that didn't obey King Obama's radical social agenda would then lose federal funding and risk becoming the subjects of lawsuits.

Talk about perfect timing! I believe Obama's bathroom "edict" was intentionally scheduled for the last couple of weeks of school, because no one had time to deal with it then. Everyone was swamped with finals exams, graduations, proms, and so forth. It was literally the busiest time of the year and the worst possible time to schedule a resistance to the measure. Because summer break was a few weeks away, people had a "we will deal with it next school year" attitude. I urged citizens to keep the pressure hot on our governors, superintendents, and city councils through the summer, but I feared it would be unlikely.

FEAR GRIPPED ME

I distinctly remember a moment around this time when God used fear to increase my resolve to be more outspoken in fighting for the next generation. Fear can be good sometimes, ya know? My children were all asleep, and I was lying in bed, reading messages and checking the news. I stumbled across a story about a female security guard in Washington, DC, who had been arrested and faced being charged with a potential hate crime for removing a biological male from a women's restroom in the nation's capital. Helloooo?! Did you hear what I just said? Let me repeat that. A security guard protecting women from men in their restroom got arrested because she kicked out a man who wanted to pretend he was a woman! The law was now giving preference to the mentally unstable man over the biological woman.

I was seriously gripped with a fear that is uncommon to me. I could not believe our culture had turned so insane and backward and that this was the country in which my children and grandchildren would live. I was livid that Obama had literally changed the fabric of our nation. I determined at that moment to be as loud a mama bear as I could over the next many years to try to help return our nation to its first principles.

This is what I posted on Facebook the next morning:

I have to admit when I saw this story last night just before going to sleep, I was scared for my children. Really, genuinely scared. How will my children survive as Christians in this country? I fell asleep calling on the name of my Lord Jesus to spare us and turn our nation back to Him once again. Please, Activist Mommies, get louder than you have ever been! At School Board meetings, City Council meetings, workplace, church . . . everyone should know where you stand! We must unite and push back this darkness now, or it will be too late.

HOW DID THIS HAPPEN SO FAST?

If you are like me, the speed with which our nation has lost its mind concerning gender is so alarming that it almost seems like a blur. I want to show you how quickly this confusion has happened once we lifted the veil of protection of God's Word concerning marriage in our country. Here is the time line:

2015

June 26   *Obergefell v. Hodges* "legalizes" same-sex marriage

2016

Feb. 22   Charlotte City Council passes Ordinance 7056, giving rights to transgenders

March 23	NC legislature passes HB2 to protect bathroom privacy
April 19	Target announces its bathroom policy based on how a person "identifies"
April 20	The American Family Association begins a Boycott Target petition
April 28	Target has lost $1.5 billion
May 4	Department of Justice issues NC ultimatum, claiming the state is defying Title IX
May 7	NC promises defiance
May 9	DOJ sues NC . . . and NC sues DOJ
May 12	Target has lost $5 billion
May 13	Obama's Departments of Justice and Education issue "bathroom letter"
May 15	Schools require trans pronouns to be honored
May 16	Target refuses to remove man (not even transgender) from women's bathroom
May 20	DC security guard arrested for making a man leave women's bathroom
May 20	NYC threatens to fine $250,000 to anyone who doesn't use proper trans pronouns
May 20	Target has lost $10 billion[6]

Look at that! In just one month, we went from Target making its public statement about transgenders in bathrooms to New York City's threats to fine those who misgender someone through using the wrong pronouns. Talk about a fast track to Banana Land!

TRANSGENDER TALKING POINTS

Like clockwork, the Left came out with all the venom and animosity they could muster to silence those of us who dared defy their politically correct and vacuous arguments with actual facts. We were called bigots, fascists, haters, homophobes . . . you know the rest of the list. Their arguments were so small-minded and petulant that I found myself behind the camera once again, filming another bathroom video against the transgender activists' favorite talking points. Here were the oft-repeated talking points we all had to endure and some of my responses to them:

"You've been peeing next to transgenders all your life."
Just because something has been a certain way, doesn't mean it should continue to be so. That's what you call an "is-ought fallacy."

"Transgenders are not pedophiles."
None of us believe being a transgender makes you a pedophile. But we all know that creepy perverts who want to take advantage of little girls will exploit this new convenient excuse to claim to be transgender and peep on females at the least, and assault them at worst.

"You are a hateful bigot."
Actually, allowing a 250-pound man to be in the locker room or bathroom with my daughter is what is hateful. So is forcing a woman who has been sexually assaulted to

endure the insecurity of showering next to a man in a gym locker room.

"XX and XY are NOT the only biological sexes."

A very small percentage of our population has legitimate chromosomal abnormalities. To compare that to what transgenders are doing is not fair. It's disrespectful to the person suffering a legitimate medical chromosomal abnormality.

"Transgenders were born that way and can't help it."

Transgenders are not "born that way" any more than anorexics are born anorexic. They both feel and believe they are something they are not. If your daughter was anorexic and said she was fat even though she was dangerously thin, would you celebrate her anorexia, or would you do everything you could to save her life? Would you assist her in her dysphoria by helping her starve? Transsexuals need therapy and love, not hormones or surgery.

They also need to know the truth: that they were not "born that way." Science confirms that.[7] And since they weren't born that way, then there is hope that they don't have to *remain* that way.

"Just pee and shut up!"

The reason I will not shut up is because this is about far more than bathrooms. The Left is very good at creating chaos where chaos does not exist and using the chaos to gain ground on an issue where they otherwise would never have been able to forward their agenda. It's a classic play out of their Marxist playbook.

If you believe the bathroom legislation battle was actually about bathrooms, let me introduce you to comments made by the transgender activists back in 2016 when this all began. Riki Wilchins, who has undergone "sex change" surgery and is a transgender activist and author of the book *Trans/gressive: How Transgender Activists Took on Gay Rights, Feminism, the Media and Congress . . . and Won*, said social conservatives and many LGBT activists are missing the point when it comes to the transgender bathroom debate. Keep in mind, this is what he was saying in early 2016, when conservatives were getting barraged with the bathroom issue right and left. We hadn't even heard the terms *binary* and *non-binary* yet:

> People who advocate for bathroom privacy *and* transgender advocates who insist boys should be allowed in girls' bathrooms and vice versa are missing a larger point, Wilchins wrote. The fact that there are even male and female bathrooms reflects that our society is structured in a "binary" way, and this needs to change in order for the full goals of the LGBT movement to be enacted.[8]

Wilchins praised transgender advocates for their work, noting they have "finally and perhaps unwittingly opened the gender Pandora's Box, and over the next few years all sorts of unexpected non-binary things . . . are about to come popping out."[9] His prediction was almost miraculous in accuracy, were it not so demonic.

The goal was always to blur all distinctions between the sexes. And they have made incredible strides doing so. It's gotten so out of hand that even some radical feminists are ticked and wondering how it's consistent with leftist ideology to have males now dominating women's sports competitions and men preying on women in their private spaces. When the radical feminists are reaching out to a vocal anti-feminist for help, as they have done with me, you know things have gotten really backward.

THE MEDICAL REALITY

Gender dysphoria has been treated for decades as a psychological problem. You must train the confused patient to decipher between reality and fantasy. I have compassion on those who suffer with dysphoria, but the compassionate thing to do is treat it, not celebrate it or accommodate it, just as you wouldn't celebrate or accommodate anorexia.

The medical reality is that people can die from mutilating themselves through surgery. Not to mention the risk of suicide. Over 40 percent of gender-confused individuals attempt to commit suicide,[10] and transitioning makes them more likely to attempt suicide, not less.[11]

Kids are discouraged by doctors from tanning in tanning beds but encouraged to transition to the opposite sex by taking drugs that are not even approved by the FDA? Aren't class 1 carcinogen sex hormones at least as dangerous as tanning beds?

Now, how is it that the medical community, knowing all of the above, would recommend transitioning as a treatment for gender dysphoria? You have to understand that sometimes medical associations take positions on issues based on ideology or financial benefit, not evidence.[12] Think of all the money there is to be made with hormone drugs and procedures to "change" one's sex. It is a booming industry right now in medicine. It is clear, looking at the statistics, that doctors who are recommending transitioning are driven ideologically or by fear of LGBT retribution, as opposed to being driven by evidence.

SHOULD WE JUST LIE?

Essentially we are being asked to lie in order to make people feel good. Should I lie and say that a person is a male when she is, in reality, a female? Should I lie and say that being homosexual is normal? Isn't it already enough that everyone is allowed to be as deviant as they wish without expecting the rest of the world to lie to them so that they can feel better about themselves?

Truth and reality and science mean nothing to the Left. People are fighting their true biological identities, and the media and Hollywood and universities are pressuring us to celebrate this! No! I'm not going to celebrate their spiritual blindness and their sexual sin. Neither am I going to celebrate their mental disorders and their resulting departure from reality! I'm going to invite them to embrace biology and who God made them to be. When people allow for anything other than biological male or female, it's Banana Land! Gender insanity is ruining our nation and our credibility as a people.

RESISTANCE FOMENTING

Most of the controversy began in North Carolina, where the state's new HB2 law was immediately challenged by the Justice Department. North Carolina immediately filed a lawsuit against the Justice Department for executive overreach. This greatly excited me, as I have been a passionate proponent of defying judicial tyranny.

At the state GOP convention in Greensboro, Senator Ralph Hise had a message for Obama and his Justice Department: "You picked the wrong state to start this fight with." I watched with great interest as many of my close friends were the very people leading the charge on this in North Carolina. Immediately, other states resisted as well.

Texas governor Greg Abbott said, "I announced today that Texas is fighting this. Obama can't rewrite the Civil Rights Act. He's not a King."[13]

Bam! That's what I'm talking about!

Texas lieutenant governor Dan Patrick said this about Obama's threat to remove funding: "We will not be blackmailed."[14]

Arkansas governor Asa Hutchinson boldly stated, "I recommend that school districts disregard @POTUS's guidance on gender identification in schools."[15]

Kentucky governor Matt Bevin issued this statement on May 13: "It is difficult to imagine a more absurd federal overreach into a local issue. Under the Tenth Amendment to the United States Constitution, the federal government has no authority to interfere in local school districts' bathroom policies."[16]

These men were taking stands that would make them very

unpopular with some of their constituents and were courageously resisting the blackmail attempts of the United States government. I have a lot of respect for that, and I thought maybe, just maybe, there were still some upright politicians in the world.

THEY'RE COMING FOR OUR KIDS!

Since we didn't crush this PC stupidity fast enough, things have gone from bad to worse. Many Americans have been thinking that, though there is nothing they can do about the actions of others, at least their families are safe from the insanity. After all, as long as we raise our kids in church and monitor what they watch and do— and maybe even homeschool them or send them to a Christian school—all will probably be well. Right?

Not so fast!

In Ohio back in February 2018, visiting juvenile court judge Sylvia Hendon stripped a seventeen-year-old minor from the custody of her Christian parents because they did not want her to take non-FDA-approved drugs to "change" her sex to male. They allowed their daughter to live with her grandparents and provided therapy for her at Cincinnati Children's Hospital. They simply did not want her to undergo this dangerous, life-altering transition. Because the child threatened that she would commit suicide if she couldn't "change" her sex, the judge removed custody from the parents.[17]

Do you feel safe now? When I read about this pending case, my blood must have reached record temperatures. I immediately started asking people near Cincinnati if they could go to the courthouse the next day to protest. But it was simply too late. The court ruling was happening the next morning, and I had just received word about it. There was no time to mount a resistance. I held out hope that maybe the parents would appeal the decision, and then we could organize a powerful resistance. My heart grieved and I prayed for this devastated family and was haunted by the handwriting on the wall for all American families in the future.

That next week, my prayers began to be answered when I was contacted by Aaron Baer, director of the Citizens for Community Values, who asked me to speak at a press conference in which we would announce legislation to protect parents from such draconian and unlawful rulings in the future.

I was incredibly swamped back home with homeschooling, home duties, ministry obligations, and writing this book, so I struggled with saying yes. But ultimately my mama bear heart was outraged, and I couldn't miss the opportunity to call all the other mama bears to action. I took my fourteen- and sixteen-year-old sons with me. I cried out in front of the steps of Hamilton County Courthouse that day:

> Our kids are ours! Not yours! Our kids don't belong to rogue leftist judges! Our kids don't belong to CPS! Our kids don't belong to lawyers who get paid to prosecute cases in which our kids are stolen from us! And our kids sure as heck don't belong to doctors at transgender clinics who profit from drugging and mutilating gender-confused children who need love and therapy, not surgery! Shame on you, greedy pigs! In case you haven't watched your share of *National*

Geographic recently, let me be the first to remind you that the stupidest thing you can do in the wild is mess with a mama bear's cub. She will eat off your face and spit out your bones. We mama bears are here this morning to tell you, if you judges, doctors, lawyers, and so-called child protection services don't get your paws off our kids, we will destroy you!

Let me tell you, I was very fired up, very loud, and very angry—without apology. If this can't get you out of your church pew and onto the front lines to wage war against the Marxist takeover, you are dead inside, and I have nothing for you but pity. We will never, ever win these battles for religious freedom and freedom of conscience, battles for the heart and soul of our nation, until we embrace the sentiments of our founding fathers, who said, "Rebellion to tyrants is obedience to God" as they launched the American Revolution.[18] Jesus's apostles stated, "We ought to obey God rather than men" (Acts 5:29).

Dr. Martin Luther King Jr. stated, "A man dies when he refuses to stand up for that which is right. A man dies when he refuses to stand up for justice. A man dies when he refuses to take a stand for that which is true."[19] Dr. King understood that sometimes there are things worse than physical death. Cowardice rots a man into nothing but a shell of a human.

FOCUS ON THE FACTS, NOT FEELINGS

How can we win this debate on gender insanity? Keep a laser focus on the facts, not feelings. We see the success of this with the almost rock-star popularity of Ben Shapiro. He is always bringing leftists back to those pesky facts.

A little science for you: XX is the sex gene combination for girls, and XY is the sex gene combo for guys. Sex organs develop in accordance with this genetic reality. Barring pathology, that's how you define male and female.

And yet, today we are told that we need to be sensitive to the *feelings* of, not only the cross-dressed man or woman, but the man with a beard and muddy work boots who thinks he's a girl and wants to use the women's restroom. And the twelve-year-old girl who protests? Well, call the tolerance police. She just needs to be a little more indoctrinated.

If your feelings say you're a pilot, we still shouldn't let you fly a plane. And if your feelings say you're the president, we don't let you in the president's quarters. If your feelings say you're an astronaut, we don't let you in the space shuttle.

If you've got a penis and think you're a girl, you're wrong. Get counseling. We aren't going to change the world to accommodate your sexual confusion.

Did you know that 80 to 95 percent of kids outgrow sexual dysphoria?[20] If your ten-year-old boy is sexually confused and wants to wear dresses and play with dolls, chances are, nine out of ten times he'll grow out of it. Puberty will actually help confirm his sexuality. He may need some help if, for example, he's been sodomized. But we shouldn't accommodate perversion. Love precludes it. We shouldn't let kids decide their sexual preference contrary to their genetic reality, especially without the input of parents. It's insane!

Feelings be damned! If you think you can jump off a cliff without a parachute or hang glider and survive, please don't follow your feelings. You'll wind up dead. If we acquiesced to your feelings, we'd be an accomplice to your demise. We can't do that. The love of God constrains us. Please, don't follow your feelings if they lead to sin and death. Follow truth.

Christians don't want to appear mean or insensitive to people's feelings, so we get bullied into submission to their Marxist agenda. Toughen up! It's time for Christians in America to toughen ourselves to some persecution and some name-calling. We are too soft. We are not warriors ready for battle. At the least sign of enemy fire, we retreat!

Stop retreating!

CHAPTER 3

THE ANTI-FEMINIST GOES VIRAL

We would not be in the mess we are in as a nation
if every Christian woman viewed motherhood
as a means of expanding the kingdom of God.

literally became famous by trolling the "vagina hatters" at the January 2017 Women's March. I know. I wish I could say my claim to fame was due to something distinguished, like finding a cure to some terrible disease or founding a charity that feeds countless orphans. But alas, I sat in my fifteen-passenger van, taped my phone to the rearview mirror, and triggered the vagina hatters, and—*voilà !*—speaking engagements, major media interviews, and a book deal followed.

It's interesting to watch the trend of society's lack of faith in the brick-and-mortar Marxist universities. People would often rather listen to a mom spout common sense from her van than listen to a paid gender studies "expert." When was the last time you saw a professor's thoughts go viral? Yet, every day hundreds of people tune in to truth-tellers who have gone viral organically, in recognition of and appreciation for their original, unfiltered thoughts. People have lost faith in the institutional elite. They'd rather hear the thoughts of a mom with ten children who has real-world experience in how to have a happy marriage and family than listen to talking heads who have a degree but don't have practical experience.

Basically, my life is one gigantic loogie spit in the face of modern feminism. If it weren't for my fierce hatred of feminism, I wouldn't be the woman I am today and the Activist Mommy might not have gotten off the ground. My videos were getting some decent viewership, but the first one to go really viral was "What Ladies Everywhere Want to Say to the Women's Marchers!!"[1] I laughed at and railed against the feminist marchers in Washington, DC, showing the disgusting maxi pads stuck on the walls, plastered with their silly man-hating slogans. I made fun of their objectifying vagina costumes and their double standard of intolerance for diverse views.

What was the response? Surprisingly, folks just couldn't get enough of it! Women were relieved to have someone representing them. People hunger for a bold, unapologetic public rebuke of feminism. I trolled the vagina hatters, and my inbox hasn't stopped buzzing and my phone hasn't stopped ringing with opportunities ever since.

When one feminist said mockingly, "I guess when all women are barefoot and pregnant, the Activist Mommy will be happy," I responded, "What are you talking about? My husband lets me wear my shoes for the outside chores. ;-)"

I am an anti-feminist. Unashamedly. Pick a modern feminist principle, and I live in opposition to it. They want to kill babies; I want to give birth to lots of babies. They want to sexualize children; I'm determined to protect the purity of children.

Radical feminists have done immeasurable harm to the moral fabric of our society. Where are the clear female voices speaking to the culture, decrying the negative effects of feminism on our marriages, our children, and our government? Where are the feminine voices celebrating the truth about womanhood and exposing the lie of feminism that's such a threat to everything worth holding dear?

The feminist lie casts aspersions on homemakers in every conceivable way. After all, how can a woman in today's society be fulfilled without a climbing the corporate ladder? How can being a wife and mother give you a voice that only a career provides? Don't you know we need degrees and titles to be effective movers and shakers? How can staying in a difficult marriage lead to fulfillment? Is there really a need for homemakers in our culture, or should we view them as we view slaveholders in the colonial era, as embarrassing figures from a dark and ugly history? Does greatness come through dying to one's selfish desires and serving others, or does it come through the fawning self-worship of feminism?

OUR WOMBS ARE WEAPONS

When my husband and I got married, we wanted as many children as God would give us. He had three more years of his medical residency, and compared to how many hours he worked, he was making less than minimum wage. We had our first child nine months and three days after we got married. We didn't have much money in those days. I would keep a tight budget in a notebook in order to make it paycheck to paycheck. My mom offered to send us a hundred dollars a month so we could afford the monthly payment on a washer and dryer. But to say we couldn't afford kids is like saying we couldn't afford money.

Children are wealth, in God's eyes. One of the reasons God makes husband and wife one flesh is because He wants "godly offspring" (Malachi 2:15). Why would we deprive God of what He wanted in our marriage covenant? Psalm 127 is one of the chapters my husband and I made sure to have read aloud during our wedding. It reads, in part:

> Unless the LORD builds the house, they labor in vain who build it. . . . Behold, children are a heritage from the LORD, the fruit of the womb is a reward. Like arrows in the hand of a warrior, so are the children of one's youth. Happy is the man who has his quiver full of them; they shall not be ashamed, but shall speak with their enemies in the gate. (vv. 1, 3–5)

Did you hear that? Children are a heritage, defined as a "special possession." They are a gift from God to us. They are a divine reward, as valuable as ammunition in a time of war. Happiness doesn't come from despising them or killing them or even preventing them from existing. It comes with welcoming them. As Jesus said, "Whoever welcomes one of these little children in my name welcomes me" (Mark 9:37 NIV).

Now here we are, ten kids later—actually sixteen if you count the six miscarried babies we have in heaven. It's a sad reflection on our culture that you can't tell folks how many kids you have without their jaws hitting the floor like you're some kind of circus freak.

Too many Christians treat marriage like a relationship for mutual pleasure and benefit, and children like nuisances and unfortunate consequences to sex to be avoided at all cost. Thanks to the impact of Planned Parenthood founder Margaret Sanger, we are beginning to suffer the consequences of a low birth rate.

THE MYTH OF OVERPOPULATION

I hear it all the time! "Ten children, woman? You're loose as a goose! That's so irresponsible!" As if I have had more children than I can care for or afford, or as if I have had my children with ten different men. The arrogant disrespect that leftists have for large families is truly a barometer of how hedonistic our culture has become.

Overpopulation has long been used as a justification for the Left to detach sex from parenthood and belittle the moral value of a strong family unit. It gives them an air of moral authority, of social responsibility. However, overpopulation is a myth. The truth is that every family on this planet could have a piece of land about the size of Texas. Much of it is green and uninhabited. Even taking a more conservative approach with your math and considering only habitable land, everyone could have at least an acre or two.[2] The earth is not overpopulated. Do the math.

Let me prove it to you further. Worldwide, every couple has an average of 2.5 children.[3] The federal government owns 640 million acres of land in the United States.[4] If you took all the land and shared it equally with the families of the world, you'd be able to give six-tenths of an acre to every family on the planet! The rest of the United States, Central and South America, Europe, Africa, India, China, Russia—all of it could be for growing food and for recreation.

The notion that the whole world is as packed as Chicago at rush hour, and that the smog in Los Angeles fills the world, and that global warming is destroying the planet are liberal myths designed to justify the child-killing tenet of their pagan religion. Doesn't it make sense that these overpopulation propagandists are also the loudest proponents of abortion?

UNDERPOPULATION CRISIS

Not only do we *not* have an overpopulation problem; we have an underpopulation crisis! According to the World Health Organization, for a population to remain the same size in the next generation, the birth rate must be 2,100 births per 1,000 women.[5] We dropped below that in 1971, and the number of births in 2017 was the lowest annual figure since 1987.[6] What this does is force our country to be dependent on foreign immigration, inflationary money printing, and/or higher tax rates for the funds to provide for our old-age benefits. For the negative effects of foreign immigration, look no further than the Islamization of Europe and the erosion of their liberties by democratic consensus!

Even worse, the percentage of births to unwed mothers continues to grow, and one of the absolute worst things statistically that a parent can do to his or her children to negatively affect their outcome in life is to let them live in a single-parent home. Thus, this low birth rate and increase in single-parent homes is probably the most predictive indicator that the death warrant for American liberty has already been signed. It would take a massive revival of matrimony and baby making to stave off the inevitable collapse of the American economy and freedom.

Isn't it unbelievable that most Christians have fallen for the Left's lies about children? Shouldn't we have a vision for eternity? We have the power to do things the angels cannot do. We can procreate! We can cooperate with God in bringing children into the world that can worship and serve Him forever! We can train warriors for Christ who will do exploits for God's kingdom. Even our miscarried children we will be able to enjoy and love one day in heaven. They make God smile, even now. Activist Mommies, you are powerful! As mentioned earlier in this chapter, if you have never thought of your womb as a weapon, you should!

We would not be in the mess we are in as a nation if every Christian woman viewed motherhood as a means of expanding the kingdom of God. There is an all-out war on the family, is there not? How do we fight this war? Redeeming the culture and saving liberty for our grandchildren's generation is not an overnight remedy. It takes time. Decades! Not to mention great patience and long-sightedness. But there *is* a way that we as Christian women can yield up our bodies as a "living sacrifice" to promote the kingdom of God and redeem our culture (see Romans 12:1). It is called motherhood!

In a recent Pew Research Center report projecting the future of religious groups, it was found that the Muslim population will grow more than twice as fast as the overall world population and will likely surpass Christians as the world's largest religious group by the year 2050.[7] Why? Because they are having more children than we are. If you haven't figured out yet why this would worry freedom-loving Americans and Christians, just read what the Qur'an says: "Fight and slay the Pagans [non-Muslims] wherever ye find them, and seize them, beleaguer them, and lie in wait for them in every stratagem (of war)" (Surah 9:5).[8] Think I'm being dramatic? Just google "pictures of Sharia law victims" and you'll find hundreds of photos of women being stoned or given hundreds of lashes for being gang-raped, Christians being flogged or burned or beheaded for refusing to forsake Christ, adult men marrying the children of their slaughtered parents, and the disfigured faces of Muslim women scarred by acid attacks from family members. I will never forget an old, grainy, black-and-white photo I saw of girls being crucified in the 1915 genocide of Armenians in Turkey. Islam is evil, and Christians are losing the propagation race thanks to birth control and abortion.

With abortion advocates killing their children and homosexual couples unable to procreate, it doesn't take a math scholar to quickly realize the writing on the wall. On the other hand, if we would have children and teach them to evangelize and engage the culture, good would conquer evil, abortion would be outlawed, pornography would be banned, and feminists would not succeed in bullying us into allowing men to use little girls' bathrooms. Wouldn't it be worth giving birth to a few more children to see that vision come to pass over the long haul?

A LIVING PARABLE

I will never forget the time we were participating in an outreach outside of a North Carolina abortion facility. There were maybe ten proabortion and homosexual counterprotesters out there waiting for us when we arrived. When we all unloaded out of our twelve- and fifteen-passenger vans, we outnumbered them ten to one! Because of our children! It was the perfect illustration of how cutting off your offspring is a losing proposition.

I am not telling anyone how many children to have, but I *am* telling you that if Christian women don't begin to procreate and treat children like the treasures Psalm 127 calls them, and train them to serve God, in forty years our children and grandchildren will be terrorized by their enemies and we will not be able to recognize the country in which we raised them.

What if you're past your childbearing prime or can't have kids for some reason? You don't have to birth a child to be a mother in someone's life. Barren women can foster and adopt and can volunteer to mentor and disciple children, thereby giving spiritual birth to Christian warriors in this world.

We must catch this vision! Our wombs are weapons against those who would overthrow all that is good and righteous about our nation. We are packing heat, ladies!

MOMS AND DADS ARE THE EXPERTS

Be very careful when someone acts like he or she knows better than you what's best for your children. This is a common elitist tactic to transfer power from you as parent to the state—a power they have not earned and will never deserve. No one loves my children more than I do. No one knows my children better than I do. No one has my children's best interest in mind more than I do. My children are the most valuable investment of time and energy I have. The Word of God calls our children "arrows" (Psalm 127:4), and we want them to be sharp. We want their aim to be true when God launches them at the target of His will for their life. We want Satan and his minions to fear their names, and the angels to long to be their protectors. With this mission in mind, it was a no-brainer for us to homeschool our kids.

WHY WE CHOSE HOMESCHOOLING

I realized I couldn't expect my kids to inhabit the promised land if I sent them to the school of the Canaanites. I was an education major, had taught in public school classrooms, and was a public school student myself, so I knew what was coming for my kids if I enrolled them in government schools. Umm . . . no thank you. So my husband and I have had to figure out how to make it on one salary, one washer and dryer, and one oven, while raising ten kids in a world that's lost its mind.

You see, I believe if my children end up lost to the ungodly reprobate Marxists, nothing else matters. I don't buy into the "all kids will fall away and sow their wild oats at some point" philosophy. I believe the way I parent will greatly affect their future choices, so it's critical to get this area of my life right. If I make tons of money, or even discover the cure for cancer, but my children are not children of God, I have miserably failed.

I love my children and want to spend as much time with them as possible. I did not bring them into the world to hand them over to others to raise them and train them. The best way to protect them against bullying and wicked influences and peer pressure is to be with them, and we guard their company carefully. "Bad company corrupts good character," the apostle Paul said (1 Corinthians 15:33 NIV). The safest place for my kids is in my home, under my protection and guidance—especially with the increasing school shootings of late! Modern public education in America is secular and humanistic indoctrination. Granted, my children learn about evolution, homosexuality, atheism, climate change arguments, and all types of leftist propaganda. But we teach them how to think through the arguments and show them *why* godless, leftist ideals are incorrect and destructive.

EDUCATION VS. INDOCTRINATION

One critic scolded me for "indoctrinating" my children. Ha! The irony of a public school parent accusing me of indoctrinating my children is somehow missed by him. Everyone is teaching their kids religious beliefs, whether they want to admit it or not. Even an atheist inculcates his child with his atheistic religious beliefs. The difference between indoctrinating and educating is that indoctrination does not give you the opportunity to analyze the opposing side.

Those who indoctrinate are frightened at the thought of their belief system being placed under a lens for examination because it cannot withstand the scrutiny. Our children have grown up hearing Mom and Dad present both sides of a debate. My husband will often take the "devil's advocate" position with our children and try to talk our kids out of their beliefs. He will make such a convincing argument as an evolutionist, or a moral relativist, or an abortion advocate, that I squirm in my seat listening while they try to formulate a reasoned and right response.

Indoctrination is what happens in public schools every day of the week. No alternative beliefs or views are allowed. How dare we teach the true history of Christianity! Some child might actually embrace the faith of Jesus Christ! How dare we call evolution a theory and allow children to also hear the theory of creation. They might actually use their brains and think for themselves. I can't help but laugh at the Left's inability to see the indoctrination the liberals inflict on a generation of publicly educated kids through censorship of all opposing viewpoints.

For years, I have lectured in public schools to lovely high school seniors in a class called "Radical Politics." They often place my lecture immediately before or after the National Organization of Women's feminist lecture. My lecture is titled "Biblical Womanhood: A Refutation of Modern Feminism." It's sad that, though the Christian faith is the most powerful historical influence on education in the West, and the Bible the most influential text, our public high schoolers aren't even familiar with biblical Christianity's refutation of feminism. Those kids are the ones who are indoctrinated, not mine. Parents of public school students have to work tirelessly to undo the damage done to their child during government school hours. I'm not saying it can't be done. I just certainly wouldn't want to take that huge risk!

Let's be honest with ourselves. A government school isn't for children; it's for the government. It's a massive, bloated, inefficient bureaucracy that too often squanders the best years of kids' lives. I believe we can do better at far less expense. And spiritually, I can keep Christ the center of my children's education. Private schooling is also an option for those who can afford it, but one must be just as careful to monitor peer interactions, as well as what is taking place in the classroom. Consider this: my husband attended several private schools growing up and said they were negative experiences for him, because the worst students who were kicked out of public schools were allowed to attend the private schools. He was exposed to a lot of corrupting behaviors in private school through the kids who were no longer allowed in the public school. Ultimately, there is no substitute for parents educating and protecting their own children. If you can swing it, please try it. You will be so glad you did!

Of course, I realize there are wonderful teachers in the public school system who are absolutely fed up with the leftist propaganda and red tape and are doing their best to make public education the best it can be given the circumstances. I thank God for those heroic teachers and pray God can use them mightily where He has placed them to impact their students for good. But increasingly we see that public schools are more and more hostile to Christian teachers who don't tow the leftist line. For instance, Christian teachers who refuse to call a "transgender" student by his or her fake pronoun or who are critical of the unscientific theory of evolution are being suspended and fired.[9] Fewer and fewer Christians are finding it palatable to remain in the system. We must pray for them to remain faithful and stand strong against compromise.

TIPS FOR PUBLIC SCHOOL PARENTS

If you don't believe homeschooling is an option for you, let me give you some pointers on how to keep your children safe in public schools:

- Know your children's teachers well. Be on a first-name basis and have their phone number or email address.
- Attend all PTA meetings and school board meetings.
- Don't become buddies with your children's administrators or teachers. Do that after your child moves on from that school.
- Read all emails that come from the school administration, and check their social media pages for updates regularly. One school district attempted to sneak in a matter-of-fact announcement of their new and very controversial transgender policy through a Facebook post, which many parents never saw.
- Network with like-minded parents in your children's school to build a watchdog coalition of mama bears and papa bears who will not tolerate leftist indoctrination and perversion on their taxpayer dime. Your mere presence will greatly assist in frightening the school administration out of enacting radical leftist policies and curriculum.
- Insist on viewing all curriculum and resources taught in the classroom *before* they are taught.
- Don't get lulled to sleep by clever terminology, such as anti-bullying resources, suicide prevention lessons, health class, or even family life class. In most instances these titles provide cover for dangerous, leftist, gender-bending, and graphic sex education.

- Know all of your children's passwords for personal devices and school accounts, and check them regularly.
- Familiarize yourself with legal services that fight on behalf of Christian students and parents, such as Liberty Counsel, Thomas More Society, and Alliance Defending Freedom.
- Involve your children in all your church, ministry, and activism activities. Helping people and fighting for what is right is contagious.
- Set aside time several times a week to read the Bible or a great Christian hero biography out loud together as a family. Make this time together vibrant and enjoyable and it will become your children's favorite time of the day.
- Be careful not to allow extracurricular activities, school, devices, TV, or work to swallow up your family time. Guard your family time with great tenacity, or other people's values will become much more attractive to your children than your values.
- Have frequent and very candid conversations with your children about their peer interactions and what they are being taught during class time.

Protecting your public school children from the harmful effects of leftist propaganda is an uphill battle. But with God's help, and through careful application of some of the tips I've listed above, you have a fighting chance.

KILLING BABIES—THE HEARTBEAT OF FEMINISM

Abortion is the heartbeat of feminism. Underneath all their vagina hats, idiotic fist-pumping chants, and provocative bumper stickers is an ocean of blood. Judeo-Christian morality, heterosexuality, and the founding fathers are all firmly in the crosshairs of radical feminism, but it's the babies that bear the brunt of their wrath and violence.

Throughout history, hasn't Marxism always spread through bloodshed? Cultural Marxism is the most prominent ethic of leftists today, and it rests entirely on the idea of challenging and supplanting mainstream cultural norms that have functioned well for centuries. And no cultural norm is a greater threat to the deception of feminism than childbearing. God forbid, getting pregnant can turn "nasty women" into mothers!

Why else would they constantly demand the right to kill babies in the womb for any reason at any time? Even when feminists are brave enough to admit that abortion does indeed kill a human, they still justify it in the name of "self-defense." Babies, they think, are little parasites that are a threat to equality and "womynhood." Why else would they guilt-trip the fertile sisterhood and constantly paint childbearing as environmentally insensitive, socially irresponsible, and unforgivably selfish?

Feminists have gotten so extreme that they're even saying that married couples having children is irresponsible. An NBC News article this year quoted Dr. Travis Rieder of the Berman Institute of Bioethics equating having children with unleashing murderous villains on the world! Rieder dares to postulate that it is immoral and irresponsible to have *any* children because of the threat they are to the environment.[10]

Feminism viciously hates any parameter-setting Deity that dares to impede their ascension out of the doldrums of femininity, but at the end of the day, they are just as religious as any Bible-thumpin' Pentecostal. They worship the created and not the Creator, as Romans 1:25 describes. There's even a movement to legitimize romance and intercourse with trees and rocks and inanimate objects in nature! They believe "Mother Earth" is dying, and one of the most important things we can do to rectify it is to sacrifice our children to the Cause. Pop the pill, and if it fails, abort the baby—it's the first and second commandment of the feminist dogma.

Let me quote from one of the most popular feminists in history to prove the point. Margaret Sanger was a pornography pioneer, birth control proponent, adulterous wife, and Planned Parenthood founder, and in her magazine the *Woman Rebel*, she said the objective of feminism was "unlimited sexual gratification without the burden of unwanted children."[11] She treated the fruitful intercourse of marriage with extreme disdain: "The marriage bed is the most degenerative influence in the social order. . . . The most merciful thing a large family does to one of its infant members is to kill it."[12] I savor the thought that I've slapped Margaret Sanger and her evil agenda in the face at least ten times by embracing the procreative beauty of the marriage bed.

In her book *The Pivot of Civilization*, Sanger promoted forced segregation, forced sterilization, birth control, and taxpayer-funded abortion as the remedy to "eliminate the stocks that are most detrimental to the future of the race," the "dead weight of human waste," an "increasing, unceasingly spawning class of human beings who never should have been born at all."[13]

It's no surprise that the largest baby-killing conglomerate in the world—Planned Parenthood—calls their coveted annual award the Margaret Sanger Award. It's not by accident that their clinics speckle the map of the United States in largely black neighborhoods. Her admiration for Hitler, her endorsement of eugenics, and her racism haven't dissuaded Planned Parenthood in the slightest from publicly venerating her year after year. If a Christian leader had publicly said what Sanger said—"We don't want the word to go out that we want to exterminate the Negro population"[14]—and had never recanted it, do you think we'd overlook that heinous racism for the benefit of the good he'd done? No way. Not so with Planned Parenthood. They have no such scruples.

Neither do the nation's most prominent feminists. Hillary Clinton said, "I admire Margaret Sanger enormously. Her courage, tenacity, her vision."[15] Every noteworthy contemporary feminist has paid Sanger homage. Her groundbreaking work in promoting fornication, birth control, and baby-killing more than compensated for her racism, her praise of Nazis, and her promotion of eugenics to weed out blacks and poor folks.

HOW WE KNOW THEY'RE LYING

I cry foul on the feminist movement. They do not really fight for the rights of females, and here are three proofs that feminists are not true women's advocates.

1. Feminists do not advocate for the lives of preborn women. Preborn women are the most vulnerable class of females in America and desperately need someone advocating for them, and yet feminists mercilessly slaughter them. Furthermore, the vagina hatters have no problem with sex-selection abortion, which results in more baby girls dying than baby boys. How misogynistic is that?!

2. Feminists do not advocate for the rights of oppressed Muslim women. Linda Sarsour, one of the leaders of the Women's March, openly advocates for oppressive Sharia law,[16] the same religion that imposes forced clitorectomies of little girls, forced marriages of under-aged girls, severe penalties for not wearing a hijab, the public flogging of female rape victims, and a host of other outrageous human rights abuses.

3. Feminists typically align with the transgender ideology, which pioneers the erasure of women in the culture. If you think that sounds like an overstatement, what do you think the end result will be of men who claim they are women competing in our sporting events? How will a woman ever win a women's marathon or high school wrestling match again? Should Title IX civil rights protections of women be given to men? If a man can say he's a woman on a whim, what is the benefit of any women's rights protections at all?

Based on these three points alone we can safely conclude that feminism is a fraud. It's a movement created to justify the immoral behaviors of women. Feminists don't truly care about vulnerable women. What feminism fights for has brought and will continue to bring more suffering and enslavement to women than the most egregious male misogynist in history.

THE GENDER PAY GAP FRAUD

Feminists have robotically repeated the mantra that women earn seventy-nine cents for every dollar a man earns for doing the same amount of work. This is one of the biggest frauds that has ever been perpetrated on our society. No matter how many times this wage gap claim is decisively refuted by economists, feminists continue to repeat it.

This is the bottom line: the twenty-one-cent gender pay gap is simply the difference between the average earnings of all men and women working-full time. It does not account for differences in occupations, positions, education, job tenure, or hours worked per week. When all such relevant factors are considered, the wage gap all but vanishes.[17]

The truth is that feminists have equal rights in America and no longer have any reason to be "marching." But, the march must go on, so they create a nonexistent injustice to achieve victim status. Never in the history of the world have women had greater freedom than in the United States right now, the feminists' marches notwithstanding.

WOMEN ARE SPECIAL

The feminist movement has worked so hard to erase all distinctions between the sexes that the culture no longer treasures women for the unique contributions only they can bring to society. Sure, men and women can do many of the same things, but there are some things only women can do. Only women can give birth. Only women can breastfeed their babies. Only women can procreate with man through sexual intimacy. To erase these distinctions is to erase femininity.

Don't fall for the lie, ladies. Embrace your femininity, and distance yourself from the greatest threat to it—feminism.

Feminism is ugly.

Feminism is sinful.

Feminism is never satisfied.

Feminism is against being feminine.

I hate feminism.

CHAPTER 4

ABORTION

We're no better than those other cultures—
the slave-peddling nations, the Nazi nations,
the Communist nations who torture
the capitalists, or the child-sacrificing
Molech worshipers of antiquity.

A n eyeball fell down into my lap, and that is gross!" Those are the words of Dr. Uta Landy, the founder of Planned Parenthood's Consortium of Abortion Providers (CAPS). Landy was speaking at the National Abortion Federation conference when she described the difficult things abortion providers must endure in their profession, like having eyeballs fall into their laps. In response, the audience laughed.[1]

Dr. Lisa Harris, the medical director of Planned Parenthood of Michigan, noted, "Our stories don't really have a place in a lot of pro-choice discourse and rhetoric, right? The heads that get stuck that we can't get out. The hemorrhages that we manage. You know, those are all parts of our experience," she said. "But there's no real good place for us to share those." She suggested granting pro-lifers many of the arguments they make in opposition to abortion. "We might both actually agree that there's violence in here. . . . Let's just give them all the violence. It's a person, it's killing, let's just give them all that."[2]

Thank you, Dr. Lisa Harris, for admitting so openly what abortion activists blatantly and regularly deny—abortion is violence against a person. It's killing.

Dr. Susan Robinson, a Planned Parenthood abortionist, said, "The fetus is a tough little object, and taking it apart, I mean taking it apart on Day One is very difficult." She used forceps to show how she pulls babies apart during abortions. "You go in there, and you go, 'Am I getting the uterus or the fetus?' Oh, good, fetus. [Robinson makes a stabbing sound effect] What have I got? Nothing? Let's try again."[3]

Awww. Poor abortionists!

These conversations were captured on video by undercover investigators with the Center for Medical Progress (CMP), and they are viewable on their website. There have since been court cases where the abortion industry predictably sued David Daleiden, the CEO of the Center for Medical Progress, in an attempt to keep these videos from being publicized. The release of these videos was an awakening for me in 2015. Not like an-alarm-clock-buzzing-beside-my-head wake-up, but a lightning-bolt-striking-the-lamp-beside-my-bed wake-up call! I always knew it was happening, but "out of sight, out of mind." Now the Holy Spirit had planted it squarely in my path, right in front of me, and I couldn't ignore it anymore.

Dr. Ann Schutt-Aine, the director of abortion services at Planned Parenthood Gulf Coast, explained to the CMP that she's often about to commit what would be considered an illegal partial-birth abortion, so she yanks "off a leg, or two, so it's not PBA [partial birth abortion]."[4]

And that's "legal." Evil, yet legal.

When we see cultures throughout history and around the world today so deluded and depraved that they legalize and legitimize things like human sacrifice, slavery, torturing political dissidents, cannibalism, or an organized genocide of Jews as in Nazi Germany, it is easy for us in the West to thump our chests and boast, "We're better. We're enlightened. We have a constitution that protects life and liberty. We believe in human rights."

Yeah, except when we don't.

I've got news for us chest-thumping, enlightened folks in the West. We're no better than those other cultures—the slave-peddling nations, the Nazi nations, the Communist nations who torture the capitalists, or the child-sacrificing Molech worshipers of antiquity. As a matter of fact, in some ways we are worse. More than a million babies a year have been butchered every year since 1973 in the United States of America,[5] and their corpses are marketed to research companies for profit.

A LIFE OF PRO-LIFE ACTIVISM

Ever since I started following Christ at the age of thirteen, I have been passionate about protecting the unborn. I remember being so excited to vote for pro-life candidates when I turned eighteen, so that I could make a difference in the lives of these babies. This was when I was still young and naive enough to trust politicians to actually do what they said they would do. How quickly I would learn how unprincipled our politicians are and how gullible evangelicals can be.

While studying to be a music major at my liberal university in Florida, I founded the first pro-life organization in the university's history. Our first semester, we hosted a very controversial and feisty moderated abortion debate. I brought in a pro-life ob/gyn, an attorney, and a post-abortive woman to sit on the pro-life panel, and worked really hard to recruit abortionists to take up the cause for the abortion advocacy. As expected, they work best in the dark, when their lies aren't exposed, so we were turned down by every one of them. The young and idealistic Democrat Club's debate team took up the proabortion cause. It was a boatload of work for a college student, but really rewarding to see an event like that to completion.

My husband is a family practice physician, which has afforded us unique opportunities to speak on the issue of abortion. We would occasionally take our family to abortion clinics to pray for abortion to end, minister the gospel, and offer help and support to the mothers and fathers showing up to kill their babies. It was always an extremely sobering experience and left you with a longing to do more to end the bloodshed in our land. There is nothing like watching a woman walk into an abortion facility (sometimes accompanied by her mom, sometimes her drug pimp, sometimes alone) to pay to have her offspring killed. It will change your life and prove to you how very real the battle is. We always felt guilty that we didn't go more frequently. We were mostly fair-weather pro-lifers until the release of David Daleiden's undercover Planned Parenthood videos.

I was watching one of the videos on my phone while I lay in bed. As I watched calloused doctors talk about their experiences killing babies, my emotions vacillated between tears of sorrow and red-hot rage.

Mark Harrington, a longtime friend of ours and the director of the ministry Created Equal, advertised a rally outside of the

Planned Parenthood abortion clinic in Columbus, Ohio. More than fifteen hundred people attended the first rally. We were going to minister outside of abortion clinics more frequently at that time, and it really bothered me that so many Christians would show up to protest when the clinic was closed, but so few would come out when it was open to try and help rescue babies.

When I discovered Mark had scheduled a second rally, I contacted him and asked if I could invite those in attendance to take a shift outside of Planned Parenthood during their operating hours. We prayed that God would raise up an army of baby rescuers who could be a witness on the sidewalks outside of Planned Parenthood every time their doors were open.

We had a sign-up sheet and were amazed to gather seventy Christians who committed to at least one four-hour shift in front of Planned Parenthood every week! Some came to just pray. Others came to just hold signs—"a picture paints a thousand words" when it comes to defending babies scheduled to die in abortion clinics. Others, like me, call out to moms and try to intervene to help them and warn them. There's a pregnancy help center right next door, and when we talk a woman out of an abortion, we walk her over to get her the resources she needs.

We show up, and God shows off! We provide the willing vessels, and the Holy Spirit uses us to wreak havoc in the enemy's camp!

HOPE IN THE MIDST OF DARKNESS

The first time we personally experienced a baby saved from abortion was very memorable. We were singing "Jesus Loves Me" with our children outside of the now-defunct Capital Care Women's Clinic near Ohio State University, when a man came out of the clinic, holding the hand of a woman we presumed was his wife or girlfriend. They both had tears in their eyes! "We've decided to keep our baby!" they announced. The dozen or so pro-lifers cheered and gathered around them and prayed for them. My husband placed a one-hundred-dollar bill in the man's hand. We prayed and worshiped together right there on that sidewalk.

A joint effort between me and my husband was probably one of the most dramatic saves I have ever witnessed. The baby's father was in his car while his mother was in the abortion clinic inside. Kneeling down beside his open window, I begged, pleaded, and reproved this man for fifteen minutes. I used every biblical, legal, biological, and emotional argument I could think of. He just kept listening. So I kept talking. He informed me that his fiancée had made up her mind. I told him that maybe he could not read her mind, and maybe all she wanted was for him to reassure her. My husband walked over and repeated that the mother probably just needed reassurance from him, and told him how much a woman loves for her man to love her babies. Sure enough, he texted her, and she bolted out of that place! Ha-ha! Take that, devil! She got in the passenger seat and hugged him and cried on his shoulder. Then we took her over to the pregnancy help center next door.

Another couple that was about to abort their baby responded humbly to our warnings and chose life for their child recently, and oh, if you could only have seen the wide smile on this man's face! He was so glad we were there. He wanted to keep the baby, but she did not. They already had five children. Their beautiful toddler was in the backseat, jabbering away. They thanked us for being there, we exchanged phone numbers, and he even asked me to come visit them at their house and gave me their home address! God is so good!

Solomon gave us some practical advice: "Where no oxen are, the trough is clean, but much increase comes by the strength of an ox" (Proverbs 14:4). If you don't want to get your hands dirty, stay out of the baby-saving business, but if you're willing to get them dirty, it's very rewarding!

One of our sidewalk counselor volunteers related a power-ful story to me. When a man dropped off a woman at the clinic and drove off, the woman immediately ran out of the clinic doors straight toward one of the pro-life counselors.

"Help me!"

"What can we do for you?"

"He wants me to have an abortion, and he'll hurt me if I don't."

She asked for a ride to her mom's, where she was counseled to gather her things and leave town.

We've been spit at, cursed, pushed, threatened, and harassed by clinic workers, police, and feminists. We've endured death threats, and the city council attempted to silence us with unconstitutional ordinances. We take all of our children to the clinic with us, and we've even had angry passersby throw things at us.

When a pregnant woman named Nadia changed her mind, little did we know how difficult her trial would be. She had already paid for her abortion. Coach Dave called out to her, "We will adopt your baby!" She approached him and admitted she would rather adopt and gave Coach her phone number.

She was at the clinic for her third "therapeutic abortion." Her doctors recommended the abortion because she had poorly controlled diabetes and kidney failure. They worried her baby would worsen her disease, and they didn't think the baby would survive to full term anyway. Nadia was torn up with guilt for killing two of her previous five babies, and she changed her mind easily. But we had to deal with her doctors always trying to talk her out of her decision.

We got involved in Nadia's life, helping her with groceries, paying some bills to try to liberate her from dependence on the kind of men that were in her life. My friend kept in touch with her by phone. The kids and I picked her up in Columbus at her house, drove her and her beautiful daughters to the pro-life pregnancy center, and set her up with a Christian adoption agency. Another one of our sidewalk counselors drove her to doctor's appointments. We had her and her three children over to our house for Christmas. Nadia finally did give birth to a premature baby, who survived for a month and a half before dying. But we saved Nadia from the bloodguilt of murder, and she was redeemed by the blood of Jesus and forgiven.

Truly, this was a joint effort by our team to love this woman and rescue her child! Coach Dave was the only one outside Planned Parenthood that day, standing in the gap for that child, but so many of us worked together to help save this baby and be God's grace to that needy mother.

Just show up, and see if God won't use you like this!

REVERSING THE ABORTION PILL RU-486

It is very common for women to regret their abortions and wish they could reverse them. Well, it is sometimes possible!

A young woman reached out to my husband after taking her first dose of the abortion pill mifepristone, also known as RU-486. After she had begun cramping, she broke down in tears and told her boyfriend what she had done. He was compassionate to her, letting her know that he would love to father a baby with her. She found my husband online and called him, wanting to keep her baby. We were worried that it was too late. He assisted her through the process of reversing the abortion pill through injectable progesterone, to reverse the anti-progesterone effects of the RU-486. Because she had already begun to cramp, it was unlikely that the baby could be saved. But we prayed for a miracle, and God showed up! Against all odds, the baby survived.

I can't tell you how thrilling it was for this mom to email us a picture of the baby to celebrate her baby's miraculous life with us! There she was, a lovely mother with a huge smile on her face, holding that beautiful brunette baby.

If you know someone who has started the abortion process and is regretting it, it may not be too late. Please send her to www. AbortionPillReversal.com or call 1-877-558-0333.

IT'S NOT A REPUBLICAN VERSUS DEMOCRAT ISSUE

Most pro-lifers do nothing more than vote Republican every four years in their feeble attempts to stop abortion. Did you know that Republican-appointed justices dominated the high court in every single major proabortion Supreme Court decision in the last forty-five years? *Roe v. Wade,* the court case that overrode state restrictions on abortion, had six Republican nominees and three Democrat nominees, and *Roe v. Wade* passed seven to two, with one Democrat voting against it! As further evidence that Republicans have betrayed the preborn babies, all their pro-life rhetoric notwithstanding, consider that Republican budgets continue to fund abortion by way of Medicaid's Title X and Planned Parenthood funding. Bush 41, Bush 43, Trump—all of them have forced Americans to pay for child killing by way of coercive taxation. Shame on us!

Planned Parenthood poisons and dismembers more than 320,000 innocent human beings every year.[6] It is unthinkable that their doors are still open!

"But don't they provide other important services for women?"

Planned Parenthood's U.S. market share for pap tests is 0.97 percent. Their market share for clinical breast exams is 1.8 percent. Their market share for mammograms is 0 percent. Yet their market share for abortions is 30.6 percent[7]—and our Republican and Democratic leaders force us to pay for it by way of taxation.

We need to move the conversation from defunding Planned Parenthood to prosecuting Planned Parenthood and their leaders. That should be a minimum standard for the pro-life movement's acceptance of a political candidate.

GOD LOVES RESCUERS

Early Christians rescued babies that were abandoned and left out in the countryside by the Romans, caring for and adopting them as their own. Christians rescued Jews being led away to slaughter in the Nazi Holocaust. Some of the Christians were captured and executed by the Nazis for their courage. The Underground Railroad, which rescued runaway slaves from U.S. marshals and their whip-wielding slave masters was managed and run by Christians, who risked prison if they were caught.

I named my tenth child Eva after one of our favorite baby rescuers, Eva Edl, a beautiful woman in her eighties, who has been arrested forty-four times for blocking abortion clinics trying to save lives. When she was nine, she and her people (the Danube-Schwabians of Yugoslavia) were rounded up by the Communists and put in concentration camps designed to starve them all to death. Her mother, who'd been kidnapped by the Red Army to do hard labor, miraculously escaped, found her daughter's death camp, smuggled in enough food to get little Eva walking again, and then barely escaped to Austria.

Once, when arrested for blockading an abortion clinic door, Eva told the judge, "Would I have wanted someone to try to rescue me when I was in that death camp? Yes. As would you, Your Honor. When I blockade those clinic doors, I'm loving my neighbor as myself."

God loves rescuers. Ministering outside of abortion clinics, we have saved many lives. I encourage you to find an abortion facility within driving distance and offer help and hope to the troubled men and women on their way to kill their babies.

CHAPTER 5

SILICON VALLEY COMES AFTER THE ACTIVIST MOMMY

You can scream at me and fight my ideas all day.
I'm totally good with that. But muzzling me
is Stalinesque and un-American.

graduated with honors from a liberal university in the '90s, when the educational elites still prided themselves in being champions of free speech and the free exchange of controversial ideas. Once married, my husband and I carried our love for debate into our friendships with frequent, friendly yet feisty debates around our dinner table about worldview and politics. We loved exchanging ideas with people. And the feistier the debate, the better! It was honestly our favorite hobby. (I know—such nerds.) We are confident in our beliefs and not threatened by those who challenge them in a civil manner.

Have you noticed recently how leftists can't handle vigorous debate? How threatened they feel by their beliefs being challenged? What happened to the celebrated practice of healthy debate? I'll tell you! Leftists figured out they can't win in the arena of ideas, so they seek to censor and silence those who can articulately refute them. To the contrary, we don't want the Left to be silenced. The more they talk, the more they twist themselves into hilariously hypocritical knots. We loooove when they talk! But when we get the upper hand in an argument, they default to cries of "hate speech" or "bigotry." We, on the other hand, believe the best solution to hate speech is more speech, more dialogue, more debate. Because the more both sides are weighed against one another, the more minds we win. We have truth on our side.

Truth is kryptonite to the Left. They flourish as long as the truth is kept hidden behind false accusations, catchy slogans, hurt feelings, and Silicon Valley censorship. Their greatest threat is a fearless individual who will not hide but will shout God's Word and God's standards from the mountaintops. If you can't be bullied (sadly, most Christians can), and you can't be bribed (sadly, most politicians can), the devil had better watch out! You are a force to be feared!

Many of my followers came to know me through one of the many media stories written about me involving censorship. In 2017, after my video against the Women's March hit twelve million views, I suddenly got banned from Facebook for three days over a comment I had made six months earlier! Yes, you read that right—six months earlier. What was really odd was that this comment wasn't even a post I had created, but a conversation buried deep beneath an old video of mine. How in the world someone even found this is perplexing, unless he or she was hunting very hard. This conversation was about what the Bible says about homosexuality, and it was very theological and very "vanilla." No name-calling. No threats. No vulgarity. Just one of those rare moments on social media today where two people are intelligently bantering back and forth on a subject in a civil manner. When I got the notification that I was banned, I chuckled at the snowflakery and waited out my three-day ban. As soon as my ban was lifted, I reposted screenshots of the comments that got me banned, warning others that Facebook has decided the Bible is hate speech. That post was quickly going viral, and within a few hours, Facebook found it and banned me for seven days. This time they were really going to "teach me a lesson."

You see, getting placed in "Facebook jail" or "Twitter jail" is the equivalent of sensitivity training, a psychological technique akin to brainwashing. By punishing me and purging Christian conservative voices from the internet, they seek to demonstrate that criticism of their sacred dogma will not be tolerated, and it will help them brainwash others into falling in line. The big tech elitists are teaching you what you are and are not permitted to speak. You have committed the unforgivable crime of refusing to be politically correct, so you will pay and you will learn, or you will be silenced. After all, we can't have little autonomous, non-robotic creatures roaming the world, thinking thoughts that resist the approved social Marxist agenda.

During my seven-day ban from Facebook, I admittedly got worried I was going to lose my platform. Facebook warns you when you get banned that if you continue to commit such "infractions," they can delete your account. My page was very new, and I only had seventy thousand followers at that point, but seventy thousand people is a lot of potential and influence, and I feared Facebook would never let me have my page back. I distinctly remember getting on my knees and reminding the Lord that I hadn't asked for this platform, and I relinquished it to Him. My page growth had been a very fast and organic growth born out of my passion to fight the forces that hate families and all things decent. I had never intended to be a public figure, and if God didn't want me to have this platform, I reminded Him that I was fine with that and I didn't want it either. I had been extremely satisfied as a busy wife and mother for twenty years, and I wasn't looking to change any of that or pursue something "more satisfying."

I got up from my time of prayer and decided to write my first ever press release about my Facebook suspension. I never have been one to take no for an answer. I suppose it's a little bit of Southern princess left in me from my upbringing and my strong, opinionated parents. Mom and Dad taught me to be a fighter. Dad fought back after back surgery, heart surgery, lawsuits, divorce, and cancer. He never gave up. He wasn't a perfect man, but his strength through adversity was incredible and memorable. Mom was a strong woman who worked very hard as a single mom and stood up to drug dealers who were preying on the kids at her after-school ministry. Truly, both of my parents were spitfires and had nothing but the highest expectations for their baby girl, who was the youngest and last child after two rowdy boys.

The press release I wrote about my Facebook suspension was a total shot in the dark, and I thought maybe my Mom and my cousin would read it. LifeSiteNews was the first to pick it up, then the *Christian Post*, and the rest was history. My Facebook suspension exploded into a worldwide story that catapulted my platform in a way I could never have forced to happen with human hands. Media outlets in Germany, the United Kingdom, and everywhere in the United States were running the story of the Christian blogger who was suspended from Facebook for quoting what the Bible said about homosexuality. The fact that in a post-*Obergefell* world, the topic of whether or not homosexuality was a sin was even being discussed, and discussed everywhere at that, was pretty amazing. My husband and kids were kind of freaking out to see my face plastered all over the internet every time they opened up a web browser, Facebook, or Twitter.

I began getting calls for media interviews from all over the nation, my email inbox was flooded, my message apps were exploding, and my phone was ringing off the hook. It became very common for my children to see Mom run out to the fifteen-passenger van with her smartphone for another media interview. Fox News. The *New York Times*. The *Daily Mail*. Everyone wanted a statement from Facebook about their "community guidelines" and whether it was forbidden to speak against the practice of homosexuality. These outlets had read the contents of my "offending comments" and were as surprised as I was that they merited suspension. Keep in mind, this was before stories of social media censorship were showing up in our news feed on a weekly basis. My story was one of the first egregious examples of big tech overreach into policing controversial speech that got widespread mainstream media coverage. Why the story interested so many people, I don't claim to know, but I think everyone was beginning to feel that a certain eerie, Orwellian, Big Brother threat to free speech was looming. This was hitting home for a lot of people on the Left and Right of the political and social spectrum.

In the midst of this story swirling around me, my family had a previously scheduled trip to the National Religious Broadcasters (NRB) conference in Orlando. This is a conference of anyone and everyone who is anything in religious media, television, and radio.

All the big movers and shakers in Christian media are in attendance, speaking, interviewing other public figures, and networking. I was there to watch my kids in the hotel while my husband went to the conference. I was not there to speak. I was a nobody. But I kept getting calls for interviews while in Orlando and would be shushing the kids in the hotel room while I took calls from the media. One night during the conference, I got an email from the NRB leadership saying they heard about my Facebook censorship story, and asking if they could fly me out to Orlando to speak at the conference. I informed them that I could save them the airfare cost, because I was already there at their conference. Ha! They were blown away.

So there I was, a nobody, onstage with Todd Starnes from Fox News, David Limbaugh (Rush's brother), and the Benham Brothers (the twins who got fired from HGTV for believing in traditional marriage), to speak about threats to religious liberty in America. I was nervous and felt unworthy to be speaking among these men and this audience. Of course, God never lets anything go to my head and is always sure to keep me humble, so when Todd Starnes called me onstage for my big moment, he announced me as the "Activity Mommy." I was trying to imagine what the audience must have been thinking as Todd invited the Activity Mommy onstage. "Does this lady make crafts?" Oh well. So much for status and reputation. Then, of course, add to that embarrassment the fact that I was wearing a knee-length skirt with high heels and was given a very tall stool to precariously balance myself upon while being sure to clench my knees tightly together so as to keep my undies from showing. I must have done the equivalent of three hundred knee presses during that panel discussion. I guess I really was the "Activity Mommy" that day!

Halfway through the panel discussion, I looked into the audience to see Christian ministry legends James and Shirley Dobson, the founders of Focus on the Family. Gulp! Were the Dobsons really listening to me speak? *Oh no! What did I just say? Did I screw up? Did I sound smart?* In spite of my nervousness, the conversation was lively, fun, and informative.

I stepped off the stage and was swarmed by book publishers and ministry leaders offering me opportunities to increase my influence and reach much larger audiences. Who would have ever thought when I bowed my head to relinquish my platform to God a week earlier that this would have been the result? It was a poignant reminder to me that the key to being promoted is holding loosely to platforms and influence and trusting God for His timing and perfect plan.

THE WIKILEAKS OF FACEBOOK

Meanwhile, in between interviews and caring for my family, I was being flooded with messages from Facebook users complaining about being wrongly censored by the social media giant. People from all over the world were sending me hordes of screenshots and evidence against Facebook. I thought to myself, *Dang! I've got the Wikileaks of Facebook in my inbox! I could seriously damage their credibility.* Now remember: this was before all the stories about big tech censorship had become commonplace in the media. Most people at this time still took Facebook and Google to be unbiased companies.

Well, it just so happened that at the NRB convention, I got connected to an actual Facebook employee who claimed she was willing to help me with difficulties I might be having on the platform. I was intrigued and skeptical, but she and I set up an appointment for a phone call when I returned from the conference. And boy, did we talk! I'm surprised the phone in my ear didn't burn up. Let me tell you: it got uncomfortable! I shared with Katie that:

- my videos didn't have share buttons
- people couldn't like/follow my page
- people would click on my videos, but they wouldn't play
- people couldn't access my page at all without the app completely shutting down
- people would like my page and go back the next day to find it unliked

One Facebook user told me, "It drives me crazy. We went back to Ohio with friends and family for the weekend, and we all tried to pull you up because I was telling them about everything you do, and none of us could access your page. It's absolutely ridiculous."

You know, you can scream at me and fight my ideas all day. I'm totally good with that. But muzzling me is Stalinesque and un-American. It's discrimination against individuals based on their political and religious views.

My two favorite little pieces of evidence against Facebook were a particular Donald Trump meme and video. This is really unbelievable. Here's the story. Someone sent me a picture meme that was posted of Donald Trump sitting in a chair with this quote beside his picture: "It's a national embarrassment that an illegal immigrant can walk across the border and receive free health care and one of our veterans that has served our country is put on a waiting list and gets no care." Just a basic political statement in support for veterans, right? This meme went bonkers viral and was shared 763,686 times! That's crazy! Well, Facebook covered up the meme with a black overlay that read, "This photo was hidden because it shows mature content, such as graphic violence." Hahahaha! So now it is graphic violence or "mature content" to make a political statement in favor of veterans' benefits? Oh, the snowflakery!

The other example of conservative censorship that just blew my mind was a video of Donald Trump behind the pulpit of a church, with black ministers surrounding him, complimenting him, and praying for him. It illustrated that Trump was not a racist. He was very comfortable with this group of black leaders on their turf. Well, to be expected, the video was going crazy viral, with nine million views, when suddenly, the video was covered with a black overlay that read, "WARNING: This video contains graphic content and may be upsetting to some people." LOL! Oh, this is really rich, folks! A video of a black rapper hanging a white boy with a noose was allowed to remain on Facebook, but black pastors praying with Donald Trump? Nope!

But the most disturbing issue I ran into by far was when Facebook started spying on my conversations inside of my Messenger app. Now, let me just pause and say I am not a conspiracy theorist. I actually mock and shun most conspiracy theories with a passion. But as sure as I am sitting here, Facebook started spying on me. Let me explain.

One night on our way to the NRB convention in Florida, we were staying in a hotel. The censorship story was going viral around the world, and everybody and their grandmother was sending me screenshot evidence by Facebook Messenger of crazy, blatant examples of censorship. Facebook knew I was collecting evidence against them. Suddenly, orange flags appeared in the right corner of all my Messenger conversations. At first, I thought it must be a change with the latest update or something, so I asked my daughters and several other people if their Messenger app had the flags in them. No one! To this day, I've found no one who has ever seen this. While reading my messages, there would be large white spaces with nothing there between conversation bubbles. I would ask the person chatting with me if he or she had just sent me a screenshot, and the person would say yes. For several days I couldn't see the screenshots people were sending me and I had to ask them to email them to me. Then the orange flags disappeared, and the screenshots started coming through again. I have all the evidence saved to prove this.

The thought of being stalked by one of the biggest and most powerful companies in the world was very unsettling, and when I first figured out what was going on, I physically started shaking with fear. I mean, I'm just a nobody. A breastfeeding, phonics-teaching mommy on a mission. I had no one big backing me, no big money, no big connections. I felt so helpless and vulnerable because I didn't know what Facebook's next move would be. I was now on their watchlist. Can you see now what I meant when I said I had the "Wikileaks of Facebook" in my inbox?

The whole thing was reminiscent of a very stressful college experience I had in the 1990s. I was typically a straight-A student getting an education degree and constantly clashing ideologically with my professors and sometimes my classmates. I would print out materials about the dangers of Clinton's federal "Outcome Based Education" program and warn my fellow education majors that not having tests, grades, and objective scoring practices would certainly lead to the dumbing down of America and discrimination against students who disagree with their teachers ideologically. My liberal professors did not appreciate me standing up to their propaganda in philosophy, psychology, and multicultural studies. I was not biting the hook, and I was vocal about it in front of my classmates, and they were done with me. But I was very studious, completed all assignments in a timely fashion, and made almost all As in my college classes.

My last semester, the education department had this odd arrangement where the same professor taught all five of our education classes that semester. It seemed to lack well-roundedness to stick us with the exact same professor for all five of our classes, but oh well. Such was the case. This professor was the crunchiest, free-love, be-one-with-the-earth hippie you will ever meet! She wore Birkenstocks, had unkempt gray hair, smelled like garden dirt, and fell asleep all the time during class. I'm not kidding you. Five stinking classes with this lady. She was generally nice, and so was I, even though we disagreed on just about everything.

Well, one day, she returned an assignment to us and she had given me a C–. Huh? A C–? I don't do C– work. After class, I confronted her and told her I didn't do C– work and deserved a good grade. She started crying and said, "But Elizabeth, you have no idea the kind of pressure I am under to weed you out of this program."

"What are you talking about? Who?" I questioned.

She said, "The people up top." She wouldn't give me names. I told her I would sue the university if necessary to protect her and myself, but that she should not allow a good student to be unfairly bullied and silenced like this. I distinctly remember that she was shocked I would offer to sue on her behalf, and she said with tears streaming down her face, "You would do that for me?"

I said, "Heck yeah! I hate injustice." She crossed out my C– and handed me my paper with an A written on it. I have no idea what ended up happening to her when I graduated magna cum laude from my university. She clearly decided to risk retribution for me, and I am forever grateful for her.

This is what the Left does. They can't beat us in the arena of ideas, because we are right. So they silence us. Marginalize us. Intimidate us. Threaten us.

I was banned from Twitter for calling out *Teen Vogue*'s digital editor for teaching anal sex to teens. Twitter has consistently shadow banned me by marking my G-rated tweets as "sensitive." Multiple petitions have been created and circulated on Change.org to get Mark Zuckerberg to remove my Facebook page. There have been countless campaigns waged by pages with tens of thousands of followers to report my Facebook page for hate speech to get it removed.

One of the most hilariously outrageous examples of big tech bias was when a page was created on Facebook called "I will find Activist Mommy and burn whoever runs it alive." Hundreds, if not thousands of my loyal supporters reported the page for the death threat, and to our utter shock, Facebook responded that it did not go against their community standards and allowed the page to remain. Ha! This was just plain and simple bias against me because I'm not one of the Left's politically correct robots. We all know a page like that against Ellen DeGeneres, for example, would never be allowed to remain. Not to mention, if I created a page like that to harass or threaten someone, I'd undergo Facebook sensitivity training through being placed in "Facebook jail." Don't let the Left fool you. They are not equal opportunists. They don't want fair play. They want us out of the game altogether.

One follower named Sara said, "Thank you so much! I wish I had your courage. I always wanted to say what you're saying and fight back against liberals and feminists who didn't represent my beliefs. But I allowed people to bully me and backed down. No more. Thank you!"

Don't look back on your life and have regrets, like Sara. Be bold and courageous and laugh at the enemy. After all, Jesus promised this resistance would happen to those who champion godly principles. He said, "Everyone will hate you because of me, but the one who stands firm to the end will be saved" (Mark 13:13 NIV).

I vividly remember the day HGTV fired our friends David and Jason Benham from their new reality show because of an LGBT smear campaign. David and Jason, also known as the Benham Brothers, are twins, entrepreneurs, and former professional baseball players. My heart sank as I read on Facebook that they had been fired, but then my heart sank one foot deeper as I wondered if David and Jason would be bullied into compromise and compelled to apologize for their position on traditional marriage. They had fame and fortune promised to them, and it was all gone in the blink of an eye. They had a very important choice to make. Would they compromise and choose fame and fortune, or would they die to their reputations and a life of luxury and continue to choose Christ?

I watched on the edge of my seat as they appeared that night on Megyn Kelly's prime-time Fox show. She threw them some tough questions, and being men of God, they did not flinch or compromise for a second. They used the media firestorm to bring honor to their Lord. They used the persecution as a pulpit to declare desperately needed and censored truths all over the major prime-time shows. It was not easy for them by any stretch. It cost them a very plush job. But they understood the words of Jesus, "What shall it profit a man, if he shall gain the whole world, and lose his own soul?" (Mark 8:36 KJV). We need more men and women in our country like the Benham Brothers, who love God and truth more than they love their stuff.

Jason and David's father, Flip Benham, always says, "Everybody wants to follow Jesus until they find out where He is going." Jesus was going to a cross to suffer and die and bids us carry our crosses as well (see Matthew 16:24). If anyone told you being a Christian would make you popular, he told you a big, fat lie and set you up for extreme disappointment. But the exciting part is, when we look to Jesus, who carried that cross for you and me, it inspires us to greatness, does it not?

Billy Graham once said, "Courage is contagious. When a brave man takes a stand, it stiffens the spines of others." Watching the Benham Brothers and Kim Davis take their stand stiffened my spine, and now God is using me to stiffen the spines of others as well.

Whose spine will you stiffen today?

CHAPTER 6

STALKERS AND DEATH THREATS AND TROLLS, OH MY!

What liberals don't understand is that sticks and stones may break my bones, but offensive names energize me.

The Left hates me. Just a few of the lovely titles they've given me are:

- redneck Barbie
- blonde Hitler
- arrogant hypocritical cow
- a blight on humanity
- gun-slinging evangelical loon ball
- demented dandruff-eating mediocrity-afflicted neophyte with glacially slow cognitive faculties

What liberals don't understand is that sticks and stones may break my bones, but offensive names energize me. I promise I could live off the energy I get from these haters and their drivel. Their antics only serve to remind me that we truly are fighting a battle with evil and the forces of darkness. It reminds me that they have nothing but intimidation and bully tactics on their side to advance their agenda, because their arguments are completely vacuous.

One particularly hilarious evening, I received the following in my inbox:

- a rejection letter from Jesus
- an invitation to hell from Lucifer
- a speaking engagement request from Adolf Hitler

'Twas a good day!

RIDICULE

The Left's obsession with childish name-calling and ad hominem attack is a play right out of the leftist playbook *Rules for Radicals* written by Saul Alinsky. Alinsky said, "Ridicule is man's most potent weapon. It is almost impossible to counterattack ridicule. Also it infuriates the opposition, who then react to your advantage."[1]

Ridicule is a powerful tool used by leftists, especially because they don't think we "nice guys" will retaliate. Leftists are ruthless and cruel. They don't share our values of kindness, love, patience, and forgiveness. They will taunt you mercilessly.

My enemies have created an endless number of bully pages and web posts to try to shut me down. There has been The Activist Dummy, The Fascist Mommy, The Activist Mummy, The Activist Mommy Annihilators, The Activist Mommy Should Be Labeled A Terrorist, and so many more. They post pictures of me with devil horns, pictures of my face contorted to look like a decaying mummy, pictures of me holding sex toys. You name it, they've tried it.

My enemies have taunted and ridiculed my husband and children. One jerk posted a picture of my teenage daughter next to a goblin and said to my daughter, "Hey just thought you should know: not only do you act like a goblin, you actually look like one." Another posted a picture of my three-year-old daughter next to a drag queen, drew on my toddler's face, and said she looked just like a drag princess. They found my husband's medical office physician directory and gave him a bunch of one-star reviews and insults even though my husband had never cared for them as patients. My haters have located and called my husband's hospital accusing us of child abuse and accusing him of medical malpractice, not because any of the above is remotely true, but simply because they want to intimidate me into silence. To try to ruin a man's professional reputation because you don't like his wife's beliefs is not fair, but it's how the Left plays the game.

I have received too many death threats to count! Thankfully, most leftists are cowards and won't actually follow through with anything crazy. However, one evening things went too far. I got two emails on the same day with similar death threats from different locations. One stated, "I wish the absolute worst for you and all of the disgusting demons you have pushed out of you. I hope they all end up gay and end up murdering you, you awful witch. You should be so f---ing ashamed of yourself you're literally DISGUSTING and I know you hear it all the time, but there's many groups against you and your address has been leaked." The other email said, "God will punish you for your sins. We all know where you live now. Punishment is near sweetheart." The fact that both of them mentioned knowing my address made it seem like it could be an organized effort. So we called the police, who came to our house and took a police report.

Some people wonder how I carry on when my children get targeted by the hate. They wonder if I worry about their safety. Of course I do. Honestly, it's one of the hardest things about what I do. And yes, I'm always calculating and praying about their safety and well-being and acting accordingly. Thankfully, most of my haters are lazy, basement-dwelling keyboard warriors who would never exert the energy to actually physically harm any of us. I can't tell you how many times they've threatened to show up at my speaking engagements, but they rarely follow through (much to my disappointment). As my platform grows, my security measures tighten. But ultimately I have to trust God, like everyone else, to keep my children safe. None of us are ever in more danger than when we are not following God's will, and none of us are safer than we are in the center of His will, no matter how dangerous the situation.

When I first started the Activist Mommy page and brand, the hate would weigh on me a little. It was never bothersome enough to cause me to want to quit, but it would sometimes sit around my neck like a ball and chain and make me feel heavy. I would have to pray that ball and chain off of my neck at times by reminding myself of the scripture that states, "Everyone will hate you because of me, but the one who stands firm to the end will be saved" (Mark 13:13 NIV).

But just as a new recruit in training to be a soldier might initially jump at the sound of a bomb blast or gunfire, yet eventually toughen up and no longer be startled, God has hardened me to the abuse and made me battle ready. Now? I laugh at them. They hate that. The devil hates it. When fear of man threatens to keep you awake at night, make the devil wet his diapers by laughing. "The LORD is my helper; I will not fear. What can man do to me?" (Hebrews 13:6).

The Bible tells us to laugh about it. "Blessed are ye, when men shall revile you, and persecute you, and shall say all manner of evil against you falsely, for my sake. Rejoice, and be exceeding glad: for great is your reward in heaven" (Matthew 5:11–12 KJV). *Rejoice!* . . . That's King James Version for LOL!

Have you ever attempted to throw liquid out of a moving car and had it backfire on you? That's a good tactic to utilize against leftists. Let their own hate backfire in their faces. It requires nothing more than simply publicizing what your haters are saying. I embarrass my haters by reposting their obnoxious pages and posts and allowing my followers the pleasure of seeing just how unhinged and fearful the liberals have become of me. I post the petitions trying to get me banned, knowing I'm risking giving them exposure, just to show them I'm not scared of them. When I do this, often the media pick the story up and the hate of my enemies is then publicized far and wide. In short, I make them step in their own poo.

When the gay porn website Queerties nominated me (along with other public figures, such as Roy Moore, the Benham Brothers, and Tomi Lahren) for the "2nd Worst Person" award, I bragged about it, posted it, and begged my followers to vote for me![2] I don't think the nomination had the effect on me that the editors over at Queerties.com had hoped.

If you run in fear or if you back down, the liberals win. If you apologize to appease them, they win. If you "correct" what you said in hopes that the leftist mafia will relent, they win. Don't ever let them win. When they attempt to silence us, we should speak louder and more frequently than before. Don't ever be silenced by them. Your voice is desperately needed.

BULLYING

I once got this little beauty of an email:

> Not meaning to be mean, but you look like honey boo boo's aborted aunt. I just wonder why do you criticize other's sexual preferences, yet with 10 disgusting broken condoms into this world I wonder if you use your husband as a chair or something. From just watching your disgusting daughter's face, I just know that she is the living proof that anal sex does produce offspring. Shove your disgusting Christian beliefs up your tired, prolapsed vagina. But anyways I think you are an exemplary christian woman . . . in a biblical sense at least in which women are nothing but brainless baby making machines. That's why the only thing you do is sit your fat a-- in a chair and complain on the internet all day and feed your pathetic inbred creatures on your free time. If it was for me, parasites like you should be sterilized.

Ha-ha! Phew! I'm sure you want to wash this person's mouth (and mind) out with soap as much as I do! Where do people even come up with such hateful, filthy thoughts? Perhaps I don't want to know. If you're like me, you find it very difficult to ever be unkind to anyone. It's just not in you to be mean when Christ has filled you with His love.

But then we get messages like this:

> You're living in a fantasy world. This is the new generation now. Wake up. Your kids someday will either be gay or have gay children. You type of people will soon die out.

See? They actually want us to die out. I'm not exaggerating.

For decades, the Left has been playing the public with a ruse that presents us as hateful and intolerant, when in actuality, they are the bullies. They have advanced their agenda bit by bit through bullying tactics because we have let them, plain and simple. Why? Because generally speaking, conservatives are good and civil people. When liberals accuse us of being hateful, we tend to recoil and back off, because we would never want to be accused of such a terrible vice as hate. We retreat, and they advance all the more. This is a costly mistake, but one we make frequently. Fifty years of being nice has won us fifty years of worsening social Marxism.

Honestly, I find this to be a really difficult topic to tackle with Christians, because Christians are so sensitive about being perceived as haters. Since Jesus our Savior is the embodiment of love and kindness, we find hatred to be abhorrent. But I'm afraid in our quest to avoid hatred, which is defined as malice, we have avoided hating sin. Ungodliness, in all its forms, is to be hated and exposed by the people of God. "Have nothing to do with the fruitless deeds of darkness, but rather expose them" (Ephesians 5:11 NIV). We are to expose darkness and call people out of darkness.

The face of contemporary Christianity is so different from the way Jesus lived that I think if He still walked the earth today, the church would unite against Him—no, worse, they might actually crucify Him! Contrary to popular belief, Jesus never once told a sinner He loved him or her (even though He did love sinners). He told people to "repent" and "sin no more" (Matthew 4:17; Mark 1:15; John 5:14; 8:11). He taught the fear of God and warned of "everlasting punishment" for sin, "where the worms never die and the fire will never be quenched" (Matthew 25:46; Mark 9:48, paraphrased). He rebuked the religious hypocrites with politically incorrect terms such as "snakes," and "whitewashed tombs . . . full of . . . all uncleanness," and warned them that they were of their "father the devil" (Matthew 3:7; 23:27; John 8:44). He took his hand-crafted whip and drove corruption out of the church, overturning tables (John 2:15; Mark 11:15–17). Quite different from the "sissy Jesus" promoted today, huh? Jesus played hardball.

When are we going to wake up to the harsh fact that leftists are going to accuse us of hate whether we choose the softball approach or the hardball approach? For example, remember when Laura Ingraham, Fox News host, got in a bit of a scuffle with anti-gun high schooler David Hogg? He demanded an apology from her and called for a boycott of her advertisers, and she made the mistake of acquiescing and apologizing to the unhinged kid. Of course, being the good little bully that he is, he didn't accept her apology and continued with his call for a boycott. So now she had angered her followers and looked fickle, and still had Hogg and the Left breathing down her throat. The latter was worse than the beginning. Don't be fooled. When leftists accuse you of hate and intolerance, they really don't think you're being hateful. It's just a tactic to get you to back off. A ruse to shut you up. Don't fall for it. Don't be silenced. Show them what courage looks like and keep on speaking truth.

SLANDER

Leftists will slander you and print libelous hit pieces about you that can cause you to lose your job or your platform, and more important, lose your good name. One hit piece against me cited an article that I never wrote, and publicly called me a child abuser! Another smear piece said my husband wants to make immigration violations a capital crime. An absolute lie fabricated from thin air. The same article claimed that we believe that a husband should be allowed to punish his wife with spankings. Another obvious lie. We did contact this publication, and since the original posting, they have since edited parts of this article and included a "clarification," a "correction," and "editor's note." But the damage was already done. The article had been shared more than sixty thousand times, and of course no one would go back and read all the retractions the author was later forced to place at the bottom of the article.

An LGBT publication said we believe it is acceptable for a man to rape his wife. Do I even have to state that this is a lie as well? All absolute lies. Liberals make these outrageous claims with no proof whatsoever, and then they link their false claims to articles written by other people we don't even know or have never heard of before, as if we are responsible for the stupidity of someone else with whom we disagree. It's truly unbelievable what people can get away with printing today, with absolutely no repercussions. I am told recent rulings on libel cases have made it virtually impossible to hold writers accountable for their actions. Our libel laws must change.

When people become so afraid of your influence and platform that they write libelous hit pieces against you, you know you are over the target. This is a dirty way to shut down conversation and debate, but that's the dirty trick leftists play. Instead of engaging me in the arena of ideas, they fabricate and print outright lies and defamation of character, using smear pieces written by the laughable "Right Wing Watch" as their sources. They sit around on their butts all day, cyberbullying good, honest people who live clean lives, all because we oppose their worldview. Take heart. The hate is all because you are winning.

AM I DOING SOMETHING WRONG?

It's easy when we are being blasted with false accusations, malicious tweets, and vulgar responses to begin to question ourselves. "Am I doing something wrong?" we wonder. Here me loud and clear. Being hated does not mean you are doing something wrong. The most loving man who ever walked this earth was hated to the point of crucifixion. If it be for a righteous cause, it is an honor to be hated for Him.

"If the world hates you, keep in mind that it hated me first," He said (John 15:18 NIV).

Now, if you are hated because you're being an idiot or a Westwood Baptist nut job, you deserve it. But Christians need to toughen up to the idea of being hated in this post-Christian culture, or you will drop out of the race. We must decide if we want to be used mightily by God to fight evil in our culture and build His kingdom, or if our little kingdoms and reputations are too important to lose. To win this battle against malicious hate, bullying, and slander, we don't need eloquence, good looks, or physical strength—we need grit! Grit is resolve, endurance, and resilience in the face of impossible odds. It takes a lot of grit to take on the social Marxists. But it is so worth it when you win a battle.

GRIT

Studies have been done on what makes people a success in the face of odds and resistance. They've proven that the greatest factor in the success of individuals was not their natural talent, their education, or money. It was grit![3]

How many of you know we will be met with resistance when we are doing God's work? Satan wants most to take out God's point men and point women, the ones who are the tip of the spear, so to speak. As 1 Peter 5:8 tells us, "Your enemy the devil prowls around like a roaring lion looking for someone to devour" (NIV).

How are we instructed to respond to suffering? Second Timothy 2:3 tells us we are to "endure hardness, as a good soldier of Jesus Christ" (KJV). It's going to be hard! In other words, "Suck it up, buttercup!" He will be with you all the way through the hardship.

Have you ever heard of Hell Week in Navy SEAL training?

According to NavySEALS.com, Hell Week is the "defining event" of Navy SEAL training and consists of five and a half days of "cold, wet, brutally" painful training on "fewer than four hours of sleep." On average, only 25 percent of SEAL candidates make it through Hell Week, the most grueling training in the U.S. military. For those who endure it, it is a landmark moment that SEALs remember and from which they draw strength during the hardships of combat.

Trainees are constantly moving, exerting, "running, swimming, paddling, carrying boats on their heads, doing . . . sit-ups, push-ups, rolling in the sand, . . . paddling boats. . . . with the cold ocean wind cutting through" them. "The sand chafes raw skin" and the salt water burns lacerations. Sometimes the trainees are so exhausted, they "fall asleep in their food."

"Throughout Hell Week," the website continues, "instructors with bullhorns entice trainees to quit," ridiculing them to tempt them to "give in to their physical pain. "The instructors make it easy, even honorable," for students to quit. Simply give up, "and enjoy doughnuts and coffee in front of your suffering former classmates."

Hell Week, the Navy says, is "as much mental as it is physical. Trainees just decide that they are too cold, too sandy, too sore or too tired to go on. It's their minds that give up on them, not their bodies." But those who can endure it are unstoppable. "They can do anything. They have earned a place as one of the elite Navy SEALs the United States sends to do the 'impossible' during times of war."[4]

During Navy SEAL training, a brass bell hangs in the middle of the compound for everyone to see. All you have to do to quit is ring the bell. Ring the bell and you no longer have to get up before the crack of dawn. Ring the bell and you no longer have to be tortured with freezing cold swims with your hands tied behind your back. Ring the bell and life gets so much easier. But you won't be part of the Navy's special operations forces. And what's more, if you ring the bell, you greatly discourage those around you. You may even cause the man or woman next to you to also ring the bell.

But if you want to change the world, never, ever ring the bell!

FLIP THE HATE

Being hated and threatened and publicly slandered is not easy, but we are made better by it. I'll never forget the time many years ago that I was going through a dark valley and there seemed to be no end in sight. I was so discouraged because there was nothing I could do to fix the situation. In my desperation, I reached out to someone who had been through something similar, and that person's words totally changed my perspective. My friend said to me, "Wow! The Lord must really love you to allow you to go through something this hard."

Suddenly my "Why is this happening to me?" turned into "Thank You, Lord, for this opportunity to grow more into Your likeness." Our temporary trials in this life should be seen as an honor that molds us into the strong soldiers God wants us to be. I am a soldier in God's army, and no matter what the enemies of God throw my way, I will not ring that bell.

— CHAPTER 7 —

WHY I DO WHAT I DO

Speaking with Josh and others like him,
I am able to achieve one of the sole aims of my ministry—
a soul won to Christ and freed from bondage and fear.
And that's why I do what I do.

My husband was working on a project around our house after our family dinner, and I was in the homeschool room with my children. While they played on the floor with Legos, I checked messages on my phone, as I often do when the day winds down and I can grab a moment to myself.

In the midst of all the emotional reactions to my vlogs and articles, Josh's message grabbed my attention. Although his words were emotional, they were not filled with the usual insults and accusations I usually get from my dissenters. Instead, I received a moving and sincere message in beautifully written prose and was honestly taken aback.

I asked my family to gather around me, and they listened as I read his email out loud. I peeked over at my husband as I was reading and could tell by the tears he choked back that he was as touched by Josh's email as I was. It read:

Dear Madam, I don't know what compelled me to write to you today and you probably won't read this but I'd like to thank you for doing these videos and bringing some sanity back to the world. I mean it as a compliment when I say you remind me of my own Mother.

I am an Irishman who lives in [the United States] . . . I thank God everyday for the United States and what it has done for the world and the principles it was founded on. My country is free from Imperial tyranny and the world is free from fascism and communism thanks to the sacrifices of America's sons and daughters. You are now the only western country that takes the threat of jihadism seriously and confronts it. However, since moving to North America I fear for the future of the West as I have seen it fall into degeneracy and utter insanity.

I will be honest with you. I left Ireland because I wanted to live in the most liberal place in the world, the west coast of North America. I have never told anyone close to me but I am a homosexual. I spent my teenage years being tortured by internal struggle trying to reconcile my faith with my affliction.

I am ashamed to say it but I rejected Jesus because I thought He had rejected me. I tried to become an atheist to remove the fear of being sent to hell. I looked at other faiths but they all condemn me. The difference is I know Jesus loves me and I felt Him try to save me on many occasions. I tried to live my life as Jesus would want me to and did the best I could not to sin and be a good, charitable Christian.

I thought I would find freedom in a godless part of the world where I wouldn't be judged for who I am. Instead I found an empty place where sin is celebrated and those who try to preach morality are bullied and ridiculed. Our society is hostile to the idea of someone trying to promote the love of Christ yet bends over backwards to accommodate the hateful and evil ideology of Islam. The Left will bully a Christian couple for not baking a cake but make excuses for an ideology that throws homosexuals off rooftops, hangs them from cranes or slaughters them in a nightclub. As I watch the world decay around me with people applauding the deviance of a pride parade, the evils of abortion or this transgender nonsense, I don't know what to do.

I know you probably despise people like me but at least you don't want me dead. At least you think I deserve a chance at redemption. If you are reading this, please can you tell me how can I find redemption? I don't want to go to hell.

God Bless,
Josh

My family and I stopped reading and prayed right there for Josh to find redemption through Jesus Christ, and for God to bless my conversation with him. Which, I discovered over the next few months, He absolutely would. Josh, in spite of the fact that he believed I despised him, took the time to consider and relate to my views and appreciate what I was trying to express. This was my initial response, followed by the rest of our conversation:

Hate you? Nothing could be further from the truth, Josh! My heart breaks for you and what you have endured, and your letter was written so beautifully that it nearly took my breath away. And to be reminded of your mother is a very high honor, I'm sure! If you were here, I'd give you a giant bear hug, cry with you, and pray with you to find Christ. That is so neat that you say you clearly recognize times when Christ has been tugging at your heart. He loves you and wants to be in close relationship with you.

Of course, I will share whatever help I can with you. I just finished a private conversation like this with another young homosexual man who was asking questions too. This is the reason I do what I do. I try to look past all the hate mail in hopes for moments like this when a sincere person comes along.

You are right. America is losing her anchor right now. This is what happens when we forsake the teachings of God's Word. It does not work! God might be giving us a revival of liberty and sanity right now, but it must be a spiritual revival if it will truly heal our divided country.

Your letter is fascinating. You are extremely perceptive and bright and seem to have a strong ability to see things as they are. That will be an amazing gift God can use in you once He makes you a new creature.

What brought you to this place? How did the homosexuality begin? Be really honest with yourself about it. Were you harmed or exposed to sexual things as a child? Does your family know you are a homosexual? Is your mother still alive? Are they religious? (Sorry for all the questions. You don't have to answer them.) It just helps me to understand, but I'm not trying to be nosy.

Redemption is so close, Josh. It's as close as you surrendering control of your life. God has taught us that if we confess our sins, He is faithful and just to forgive us of our sins and cleanse us from all unrighteousness. ALL unrighteousness . . . drunkenness, drugs, lies, blasphemy, sexual sin. All washed away by His sacrifice for us. He also said to seek Me and you will find Me. Knock and the door will be opened to you. He said to call upon the name of the Lord and be saved. He said to confess AND FORSAKE our sins and we will find mercy.

It's 2:43 in the morning and my baby has wakened for me to feed her. So let's start with this and keep talking. ok? Praying fervently for you! God bless.

Elizabeth

* * *

Thank so much for replying! My apologies if I woke you, my cousin who lives in Boston told me he doesn't get to sleep anymore since they had their baby. I don't know how you cope with 10!

With regard to your questions, yes I still have my parents, my mother and all my grandparents are very religious but my father has no faith. I believe this is mainly due to his negative view of the Catholic Church and the clerical abuse scandals in Ireland. I had a fantastic upbringing and never suffered any kind of abuse. I feel very blessed to have the family I do. I started to have these feelings around puberty the same time my peers were. My family does not know as it would break their hearts and I would shame the family.

Thank you for trying to help me. I really appreciate you showing me true Christian compassion. May I ask your name or how you would like to be addressed?

God Bless
Josh

* * *

Glad to hear you have a lovely and supportive family. ❤ *Do you have a Bible? And I guess also . . . do you believe the Bible is God's message to us?*

I hope you don't allow abuses in Catholicism to turn you away from the beauty of Jesus. He is not at all like the priests who have lied and abused people. He is always trustworthy and good and holy.

Elizabeth

* * *

I gave my Bible to my brother at Christmas but I will get another one. I have actually finished reading the Quran and Sunna which strengthened my faith in Jesus. I know Jesus alone is the example we should follow.

Josh

* * *

Hey Josh!! We have been traveling out-of-state this weekend for a speaking and singing engagement with our 10 kids. Been a bit hectic. So sorry I haven't reconnected with you yet. Thanks for your patience. I will try to email you tomorrow. Ok? Been praying for you!

Love and blessings in Christ,
Elizabeth

* * *

Hey Mrs. Johnston! No worries at all! I can't imagine how busy you must be, to be doing everything you are doing and raising such a big family as well. I really appreciate your help in any way you can and don't worry about responding on any kind of timeframe. I am just grateful to have someone to talk to.

I hope your speaking and singing engagements were successful and you were able to spread your message. I look forward to hearing from you.

God bless,
Josh

* * *

Hey Josh! Thanks for understanding about my tardiness. How are you? Anything new? Have you gotten your hands on a

Bible yet? If not, here is a link. May I recommend you begin by reading the book of John, written by one of Jesus' closest disciples? Here are the first two chapters of that book. It's beautiful.

Ask me any questions you might have about the Bible or life or whatever. We want to be here for you however we can to lend support. We love and pray for you.

Blessings in Christ,
Elizabeth and family

* * *

Hi Josh. Just checking in. You doing okay?

Elizabeth

* * *

Hi Mrs. Johnston. I had a few rough days but back on track now. I read the Scripture and recall studying this before. . . . The example of Jesus was always my favorite part about studying the Bible. I feel many people who call themselves Christian don't follow the example of Jesus.

How is everything going with you? Do you tour around the states often?

God bless,
Josh

* * *

Yes, you are right. Many so-called Christians do not live like Christ. It is sad. Just like you might be able to identify with the dilemma of people in the gay community who give gays a bad name. Keep your eyes on Jesus, not necessarily those who claim to be His followers. Redemption comes through a relationship with Him. Are you ready for that? Are you in a relationship with a man right now?

Love and prayers,
Elizabeth

* * *

No, I have never been in a relationship and only tried to meet others like me when I came to [location] but I avoid that now. I just want to have some close friends and that's all. Do you think I will be able to change my orientation or will Jesus be forgiving if I just stayed away from that environment all together?

Josh

* * *

Hi Josh. All Jesus wants is your heart. He will take care of the rest and make you a new creation. If you are ready to begin that journey, I want to encourage you not to hesitate.

You don't have to do anything to "get your act together" first. Just call upon the name of the Lord, repent of your sin, and be saved.

I would like to ask you to do something for me. I have a friend who leads a ministry where several of the people on staff are former homosexuals. I feel like they could really help you since they have somewhat walked where you have. Here it is . . . Janet Boynes Ministries. Janet herself was a homosexual before she surrendered to Christ. Would you reach out to them on Facebook?

Sorry it took me so long to get back. Things have been crazy. I got banned from Facebook for a week because of speaking what the Bible says about homosexuality. Praying for you, friend.

Elizabeth

* * *

I would love to do that and I am ready to call upon Jesus. I really appreciate you going to all this effort, you didn't have to do any of this and I want to thank you for your compassion.

That's crazy that Facebook did that to you. The Left is really starting to scare me with their censorship and authoritarianism.

Thanks again.
God bless,
Josh

* * *

Yes, the censorship is getting way out of hand! My FB suspension is a huge national news story right now . . . Fox News, Drudge Report, New York Times . . . crazy!

Josh, I am so excited that you are ready to begin the most wonderful journey of your life. To have peace on the inside (regardless of what is going on in your life) . . . there is nothing like it! Let us know if you ever want to try to meet up or skype. It is imperative to read God's Word and find a good church that teaches the Bible without fear.

Have you had a chance to reach out to Janet Boynes Ministries on Facebook yet?

Elizabeth

* * *

I just read all about it, thank God you were vindicated. I have reached out to Janet and am awaiting a reply. I will let you know how everything goes. Thank you so much for your help.

God bless,
Josh

* * *

Happy Thanksgiving Elizabeth! Thank you for your message. Life is going great at the moment. I am like a new person and God is pushing me in the right direction. I haven't touched alcohol in 6 months and my sister is coming to live with me before Christmas. Hope you and your family are well and enjoy the holidays.

God bless,
Josh

My conversation with Josh is a side of the Activist Mommy that few get to see. Speaking with Josh and others like him, I am able to achieve one of the sole aims of my ministry—a soul won to Christ and freed from bondage and fear. And that's why I do what I do.

CHAPTER 8

TEEN VOGUE BITES THE DUST

*Sometimes I just want to tell leftists to
go hug a tree and shut up while we clean up
the mess they've made of our country!*

everal of my followers were first introduced to me through my very public tussle with *Teen Vogue* magazine. During the summer of 2017, several people sent me an article published by *Teen Vogue* and written by Gigi Engle entitled, "A Guide to Anal Sex; How to Do It the Right Way." I mean, we all already knew most of the teenage mags like *Teen Vogue* are a bunch of leftist trash, but really? A teen fashion magazine, which markets its content to teenagers between the ages of twelve and eighteen, teaching kids anal sex like it's no big deal? Are you even kidding me? As a mom of ten children, whom I do my best to protect from sexualization and immorality, I was livid. Who do these raunchy people think they are?

Just think about it. You've got adult editors selling anal sex in the most graphic terms to underage children. If an adult had texted or spoken the words in that article to a thirteen-year-old, he or she could be prosecuted. But Gigi Engle and *Teen Vogue* can publish obscene advice for teenagers worldwide, and no one blinks an eye. The content of the article is so graphic I can't even include it in my book for adults, but one of the milder statements in the article was, "Anal sex and anal stimulation can be awesome, and if you want to give it a go, you do that. More power to you."[1]

Hmm. Gigi forgot to mention the list of health risks that go with indulging in anal intercourse, the loss of bowel control, hemorrhoids, anal fistula and fissures, rectal ulcers, rectal prolapse, and I could go on. She forgot to mention that condoms have never been approved by the FDA for anal intercourse. And she forgot to mention that former surgeon general C. Everett Koop said "people should never engage in anal intercourse, even if using a condom. 'Anal intercourse is simply too dangerous a practice' because it tears the lining of the rectum and thus provides a point of transmission for the [AIDS] virus, Koop said."[2] "Condoms provide some protection, but anal intercourse is simply too dangerous to practice."[3] Gigi also failed to mention that anal sex is the riskiest sexual behavior for contracting and transmitting HIV for men and women, according to the CDC.[4] Oops! Just a few innocent omissions, right?

As if the article itself, which still remains online to this day, is not reckless enough, this obscene piece didn't even include the precautionary "safe sex" instruction you would expect from a leftist when discussing such a risky sexual practice. This glaring omission even outraged liberal parents. It wasn't until after *Teen Vogue* came under intense public criticism that they edited the article to include any precautions.

I stewed all day over this outrageous anal sex tutorial. What could I do to make a difference? How could I draw the most attention possible to this disgusting excuse of a publication and make them pay for pandering obscenity to minors? My family and I went out to eat that night, and I told them, "When we get home, if it's not too dark, I think I'm going to film myself burning a *Teen Vogue* magazine." My husband was all in, because he's a borderline pyromaniac, so any excuse to build a fire is a good excuse, especially when it includes burning some certified smut. My teenage kids weren't so sure. I really value their opinions and often take their advice. They were a little concerned it would come off as cheesy and flop. Frankly, I was concerned it would flop too. But the situation was so outrageous that it called for a dramatic response. I decided to take the risk.

When we got home from dinner, I asked my husband if he would build me a little bonfire in the backyard fire pit. While he did that, I freshened up my lipstick, lamenting how bad I looked that night, and grabbed my selfie stick for filming outside. I had no idea what I was going to say and just started filming and "let it rip" with no preparation. It was short and sweet—only two minutes long. While I burned the magazine, I said, "These editors' brains are in the gutter. Now let's put their sales in the gutter where they belong." I asked parents all over America to speak to their local storekeepers, library managers, and bookstore owners to ensure that they pull *Teen Vogue* from their shelves permanently.

THE MEDIA FIRESTORM

I posted the video and thought, *Meh. Probably won't be seen by that many people.* But then I checked my page about thirty minutes after posting it and—holy guacamole!—This was the fastest-moving video I had ever posted, even faster than my Women's March video that got twelve million views. It turns out that parents really weren't very tolerant of twenty-something-year-old authors teaching kids how to sodomize one another. Parents, both conservative and liberal, were rightly outraged, and we launched Operation Pull *Teen Vogue*.

I watched the video climb from one million to five million

views in just a few days, then to ten million, and to date it's been viewed more than fifteen million times![5] I began getting calls for tons of radio interviews, even as far away as the UK, to discuss the sexualization of children in our culture. It was a great opportunity to expose how obscenity laws are not being enforced in our nation. I honestly had no real hope that we would bring *Teen Vogue* down, such an industry giant, carried by Condé Nast (who also carries *Vogue, Vanity Fair, GQ, Glamour,* and *Brides* magazines). Even so, I was certainly going to have fun trying.

There were so many stories written in the mainstream media about our little grassroots Operation Pull *Teen Vogue*:

- "Activist Mommy Starts 'Operation Pull *Teen Vogue*' after Mag Peddles Perversion to Minors"[6]
- "'Activist Mommy': *Teen Vogue*'s Guide Would Be Crime If Texted to Minors"[7]
- "'Activist Mommy' Claims *Teen Vogue* Broke the Law with Its Anal Sex Article"[8]
- "Parents Outraged over *Teen Vogue* Anal Sex How-To Column (but Magazine Still Defends It)"[9]

Even Rev. Franklin Graham wrote about it on social media and asked parents to join Operation Pull *Teen Vogue*![10] Whoa!

THE PARENTS GET IT DONE!

I tried to recruit large Christian activist organizations with a résumé of successful boycott campaigns to get behind Operation Pull *Teen*

Vogue to help me start contacting *Teen Vogue*'s advertisers, but they did not join the effort. So, as usual, I was going to be fighting this battle without the powerhouse conservative organizations, but side by side with the greatest audience in the world! I could have never done it without my awesome audience. I love my followers! They are bulldogs. They love to get stuff done. And they are fiercely loyal to the Activist Mommy, or TAM, as they often like to call me. I started getting very encouraging messages sent to me, like this one:

> I went into my local Kroger, grabbed all 9 mags on the rack. I walked right up to the manager and asked him if he would allow his kids to read this. No joke folks, he (the manager) literally ripped them up and told his loss prevention team to write them off as stolen. I'm now shopping there for the rest of my life.[11]

Ha! I love it! This is the kind of righteous indignation that must be revived if we hope to save this nation from the progressives in power who are sexualizing our children.

My audience and I began to research and post *Teen Vogue*'s advertisers' phone numbers and email addresses and warn them that they were advertising with a publication that teaches kids how to sodomize one another. We told them we were very angry about *Teen Vogue*'s reckless promotion of promiscuity and sodomy and that we were notifying the public of their advertisers.

Is marketing this kind of sexual content to teens even legal?

Our obscenity laws are good and on the side of decency. Section 1470 of Title XVIII of the United States Code specifically prohibits "any individual from knowingly transferring or attempting to transfer obscene matter using the U.S. mail or any means or facility of interstate or foreign commerce to a minor under sixteen years of age."[12] Convicted offenders face fines and imprisonment for up to ten years. Did you read that? Then why the Sam Hill are magazines like *Teen Vogue* not being prosecuted for pandering obscenity to minors? This is the question I asked while being interviewed on nationwide radio shows and printed publications.

TEEN VOGUE'S PROVOCATIVE RESPONSE

Phillip Picardi, then digital editorial director of *Teen Vogue*, responded on Twitter to Operation Pull *Teen Vogue*: "The backlash to this article is rooted in homophobia. It's also laced in arcane delusion about what it means to be a young person today."[13] Oh, I'm sorry, Phillip, I didn't realize being a young person today automatically included the most dangerous kind of sexual activity possible. Phillip's tweet tirade ended with a picture of him and his homosexual boyfriend kissing while he shot all of us concerned parents the middle finger with a rainbow-polished fingernail. I guess that's how they handle customer service issues over there at *Teen Vogue*.

Something was clearly very wrong over at *Teen Vogue*, and we kept exposing them at every turn for their peddling of perversion and lack of journalistic integrity. We caught them peddling sex toys to kids and reminding children not to forget their tubes of sex lubricant in their school backpacks.[14] We kept hammering them with bad press and exposing their perverted agenda. This continued for months, with no hope of *Teen Vogue*'s downfall in sight.

THE OH-SO-PREDICTABLE BACKLASH

Boy, did the name-calling and bashing begin! The filth and vitriol that came at me on social media, especially Twitter, was almost suffocating. I could never reprint it. It's much too filthy. But some of the milder accusations were that I was "a homophobic bigot who wants LGBT kids to be bullied," simply because I didn't believe *Teen Vogue* should be teaching kids how to be "safely" sodomized. I was a "Nazi book burner" and an "authoritarian, blonde Hitler" for wanting people to exercise their powers of free speech via a boycott of the magazine.

I just had to chuckle about that one, because it seemed to be lost on the leftists that a boycott is a form of free speech whereby people express their beliefs by the way they spend their money. It's called free enterprise and is a great American ideal.

Some were actually employing the "free speech" argument to defend *Teen Vogue*'s anal sex tutorial. Pandering obscenity to minors, however, is NOT protected free speech! Free speech does not protect someone as he or she disrobes and has sex in front of my kids. It is a prosecutable crime. If lawmakers and law enforcement won't enforce the law, then sometimes we the people have to go to the storeowners and demand they pull the obscenity from the shelves. Sometimes we are forced to hit companies in the pocketbook when they refuse to listen to the concerns of the people, just as we did at Target, resulting in a $15 billion loss for the corporation (see chapter 2).

Don't you just love the ideals of those on the Left? Leftists want to be outraged over the immorality of air pollution or a Christian woman burning a magazine, but they think it's perfectly okay to teach children how to have anal intercourse! Sometimes I just want to tell leftists to go hug a tree and shut up while we clean up the mess they've made of our country! Unbelievable!

SHOULDN'T YOU USE A SOFTER APPROACH?

But the Left weren't the only ones with criticism. I would be remiss if I didn't mention the token criticisms I got from nicer-than-Jesus Christians who thought my burning of the *Teen Vogue* magazine and calling for a boycott was a bit too confrontational and maybe "not what Jesus would do." Ha! This was my response to them on Facebook:

> *I am more than happy to figuratively or literally burn things that are a threat to my children and other's [sic] children. This is WHY almost half a million people follow me. People are sick of the bend-over-and-take-it-version of Christianity that intimidates Christians into silence and obeisance to the sexual agenda of the Left. Nope. Not gonna do it. There are decency laws in our country that are not being enforced, but should be enforced. I care about kids and am going to make sure those laws are enforced. You go ahead and sit on your butt and be content to "just don't buy it." I'm going to actually*

do something about it and will only wear your criticisms as a badge of honor that I'm doing something right. For those of you who think calling people out who are pandering obscenity to minors is "aggressive," don't let the computer hit you on the butt as you unfollow my page. I have ten children. I am a mama bear. This is what mama bears look like when cubs are being attacked and sexually assaulted . . . a little "aggressive." I'm proud of it. It's what makes me The Activist Mommy.

Criticism from the Left is expected, but the criticism from your own is what can gnaw at you. You have to be really confident in what God has called you to do to stand firm in the midst of criticism from your own.

A VERY GOOD DAY

November 2, 2017, was a very good day. I woke up and peeked at Twitter on my phone and saw people trying to get my attention by tagging me in a particular tweet. It read in all caps, "TEEN VOGUE IS DEAD" and was accompanied by an article entitled, "Condé Nast to Cease Teen Vogue in Print, Cut 80 Jobs and Lower Mag Frequencies." What? Did I really just read that? Is it possible? Did we really give *Teen Vogue*, a publication that has been in print since I was a little girl, such a black eye that they will never recover from it?

I read everything I could find to verify the facts. Sure enough, out of all the publications that Condé Nast carries, the only one going out of print was *Teen Vogue*.[15] What a shocking coincidence!

So, it wasn't just an inevitable move toward digital in this digital age, because none of the other Condé Nast magazines being read by young women were going out of print. Only *Teen Vogue*.

I told my kids, who were super excited, and I shared the victory with others on social media and fielded interviews. For instance, the *Christian Post* printed an article entitled, "'Activist Mommy' Hails Victory After Condé Nast Halts Teen Vogue Print Edition."[16] Of course, *Teen Vogue* stayed completely silent and refused to comment. We all knew no comment was necessary.

GOD CAN USE WEAK THINGS

I'm just one person, and I'm just like you. I'm a busy homeschool mom and have a lot on my plate. I like to get stuff done, not just talk about it, and sometimes that requires controversy, confrontation, and yes, even fire. But if you're willing to get a fire started, you'll be amazed how many people will find you and keep the fire going.

God can use one small person in a powerful way. I received an email from a mom who was asking for prayer and help. She had watched my *Teen Vogue* video and was outraged. She went to work calling her friends and all the local stores and even called her local news station. Fox local interviewed her and ran a story on it. And because of her phone calls, her representative called her to ask how she could help with Operation Pull *Teen Vogue*. I could tell she was nervous, and she left her phone number in the email, so I called her and prayed with her. She was on fire and so excited about how God was using her. It's the greatest honor to watch others catch the vision and run with it. And boy—did that ever happen a few months later through a movement that started as a mere grassroots disturbance of moms and dads who were sick of schools teaching their kids how to be sexually promiscuous!

OUR SEX ED MAMA BEAR MOVEMENT
THAT WENT GLOBAL

Something very organic that I never expected would happen through the growth of this platform is that followers have begun sending me concerns and battles of all types to fight. Once I received an email from an airline captain who was appalled about an obscene advertisement he saw playing on all the television screens around the airport. People send me information all the time, pleading with me to expose some particular evil or help them with this or that. Of course, there is only one of me and only so much I can do. I receive more email with more concerns than I can possibly tackle by myself. However, one particular threat to children kept popping up in my inbox so regularly, I knew I had to jump on it! Parents were outraged by the pornographic sex ed they were finding in their children's school classrooms, with the blessing of the administration. Kids were being taught how to masturbate, have orgasms, pleasure their partners, have anal and oral sex, and the disgusting list goes on and on! As a homeschool mom, it might be easy to ignore this public school issue, but my heart broke for the parents who felt stuck in the system and powerless to stop the raping of their children's minds.

I got fed up with hearing parents complain about it and decided to do something about it. I picked a fight with one of the largest and most powerful bureaucracies in our nation: the public schools. I ran my idea of a "sit out" by some mom friends of mine to get their thoughts, and they all agreed that something needed to be done—and quickly! We picked a date in April and launched Sex Ed Sit Out. We were only going to organize a sit out in one city, since we had no resources. But in a couple of short months, the mainstream media picked up the story, and it grew into a global movement in four countries. Did you hear that? Four countries!

Family Research Counsel, Liberty Counsel, American Life League, and so many others ended up partnering with us. Rush Limbaugh talked about us for over an hour on his show. Franklin Graham, whom I've never had the honor of meeting, encouraged parents to sit out with us in protest! I was on the phone nonstop taking media interviews and had to start delegating some of the interviews to other moms.

My critics said a one-day sit out wouldn't make a difference, but I've received messages from multiple parents from California to Canada saying that at least 60 percent of their school sat out on April 23, 2018, for Sex Ed Sit Out. One mom in Sacramento wrote to tell me their school lost more than *one hundred thousand dollars* that day because of the Sex Ed Sit Out. Her brother-in-law was on the parents board and was so angry at her for mobilizing parents that he wouldn't even speak to her.

You see, for every day a child misses school, the school loses federal dollars. That is why we chose this strategy. If school boards and administrators were going to completely ignore the clearly expressed wishes of parents, we were going to hit them in the pocketbook, which is what seems to speak most loudly when you are dealing with bureaucrats. We exposed in very graphic terms, on social media through our Facebook page and website, what Planned Parenthood and Human Rights Campaign were teaching in our schools. We weren't polite or proper about it. And it worked. The mama bears awoke from their dens of hibernation and started fighting back!

Parents are now confronting their administrators and getting the graphic, gender-bending curriculum thrown out. And many of them are homeschooling today because of Sex Ed Sit Out. I bumped into one mom in Charlotte, North Carolina, who told me she is homeschooling her children now as a result of Sex Ed Sit Out, and I've received many similar messages online.

One of the most powerful things we did was threaten to sue the schools for pandering obscenity to minors. Now we are hearing of such lawsuits popping up all over the country by parents and organizations such as Liberty Counsel. One Chicago mom, named Sally Wagenmaker, got a restraining order against a porn star and sex expert who was being snuck into her kid's school to rape the minds of those children.[17]

Yes! I love it! It's past time for us to get aggressive and go on the offensive for once. Why are we always on the defensive? "The earth is the LORD's, and the fullness thereof" (Psalm 24:1 KJV). He has dominion over it, and we are His ambassadors. Let the slimy Marxist degenerates who are determined to sexualize our kids go running back into their closets where they belong. They should fear being caught. They certainly shouldn't be invited into our schools, funded by the taxpayers!

One little person with a really big God can do so much! When I made that bonfire video, I had absolutely no idea the fire it would set. I am truly humbled and honored to be a part of exposing evil, protecting children from sexual exploitation, and emboldening parents around me. I couldn't do it without my audience being behind me 100 percent. Together, my audience helped me shut down *Teen Vogue*'s print magazine, shut down sex brothels, get perverted Facebook pages deleted, and launch a global movement to protest graphic sex education in public schools. Together we are winning the battle against the hedonistic secular humanists, and together we will keep winning!

CHAPTER 9

THE INTENTIONAL MARXIST TAKEOVER

*The push for big government, the sexualization
of our children, the erosion of parental rights,
and the weakened family unit is not accidental or even
a natural progression of living in an enlightened society.*

What has happened to America? How has it come to this? It was the Roman poet Juvenal who first coined the term *bread and circuses* when he wrote, "Two things only the people anxiously desire—bread and circuses."[1] Thence comes the iconic image of drunken crowds in the Roman coliseum, crying out for the loaves of bread that were enthusiastically tossed to them in intermissions between bloody battles.

BREAD AND CIRCUSES

Bread and circuses represents the failure of the thoroughly entertained and well-fed Roman citizens to defend the liberties of the Roman Republic. Rome went from freedom and democracy in 133 BC to a massive tyrannical central government by the end of the first century AD. And that is right where we are headed in America.

What did freedom look like in America 230 years ago? Literacy was 97 percent in Thomas Jefferson's study of American education[2]—the first of its kind. Since then, we've ranked in the bottom of the list of industrialized nations in math and science. Presently, the average American works from January 1 to mid-April for the government, upon pain of fine, prison, or property confiscation.[3] We've killed off one-sixth of our population in four and a half decades through abortion.[4] We have the highest imprisonment rate in the world.[5] With federal spending at $12,000 per person[6], we have one of the most expensive governments in the world—not even counting the cost of state and local government. With a federal debt over $20 trillion and growing,[7] every single American owes $62,500,[8] yet the median household income is about $10,000 less than that.[9] It is a debt we and posterity could never repay, even with the Federal Reserve printing trillions of dollars a year. The best minds think a dollar collapse and massive correction with immense suffering is impossible to avoid. Don't be tricked by the bread and circuses—we are far less free than we were 230 years ago.

Our great-great-grandparents knew freedoms we can't imagine. They could have never fathomed that so much of what they handed down to us would be lost! How was it lost?

Bread and circuses were part of the plan. And it was definitely a plan.

Bread

Government welfare. Never have more Americans been dependent on the government's bread to survive. In 2011, 49.2 percent of U.S. households received benefits from one or more government programs. Thanks to Obamacare and Medicaid signups, that's roughly 52 percent now.[10]

A wise man once said, "When the people find that they can vote themselves money, that will herald the end of the republic."

And it's not by accident. FDR, who dreamed up the massive welfare state, said this about the payroll contributions workers make to Social Security: "We put those payroll contributions there so as to give contributors a legal, moral and political right to collect their pensions. With those taxes in there, no d—n politician can ever scrap my Social Security program."[11]

He was right. Even fiscal conservatives fight for the right to keep their bread when they've been fooled to think they've paid into the program with every paycheck. You know those limited-government conservatives on the campaign trail? They grow the welfare state just like the Dems! You're more likely to see Ron Paul in a casino than you are to see a Republican oppose a government welfare program. The fish is hooked and the string is strong. It's just a matter of time.

We are lethargic and morbidly obese on the government's bread. Unfortunately, the siesta lasts only as long as the government can get away with counterfeiting money and diluting the value of the dollar. How long until those who invest in the dollar grow fed up with us devaluing the value of their holdings? How long until those who invest in the dollar are prompted by malicious motives to turn the tables on us, as the lenders are inclined to do to their debtors from time to time? "The borrower," the Bible says, "is slave to the lender" (Proverbs 22:7 NIV).

Don't be fooled by all the bread. Our kids and grandkids will pay for it in the currency of chains.

Circuses

Entertainment. Dawn till dusk. Never have Americans been so drunk with pop culture, movies, TV, video games, sports, reality shows, and social media. We are intoxicated with the circus beer.

My husband and I decided long ago that we weren't going to have a television in our home. We were raised in front of the TV and were determined that our children would have a different life. One of the most common questions my husband and I get is "How do you two get so much accomplished?" I often answer, "We don't have cable TV."

We want to be readers and workers, not couch potatoes. But your average Christian is entertained into lethargy, dawn to dusk. No time for outreach, volunteering, Bible study, prayer, and righteous protest. No time.

Never has our society been more addicted to screens, now that most of us are carrying smartphones in our pockets 24/7. Like bait on the mousetrap, bread and circuses are distractions that are necessary for the government's violent clampdown on freedom. And it is fast approaching.

"WOKE CULTURE"
IS MORE "WOKE" THAN US

Ever heard the term *woke*? It's an urban word that refers to being aware of social justice and racial justice issues. "Stay woke!" they like to say.

Christians and conservatives aren't aware how far the social Marxist clamps have suffocatingly closed around us already. We aren't as "woke" as elementary kids in your average public school. We think if the bills are paid, kids are fed, church doors are open, and Republicans are getting elected, everything's fine. We are oblivious to what's really happening around us and just how intentional it all is.

Just check out these recent developments:

- Hollywood just awarded an Oscar to a movie about man-boy love, *Call Me By Your Name.*
- A proposed law in Delaware would allow kids to change their gender or race without notifying parents.[12]
- A website called Transkids sells kid-sized penile prosthetics to gender-confused children.[13]
- The Ohio courts just stripped a seventeen-year-old daughter away from her Christian parents because the parents refused to permit her to ingest hormones to undergo a sex change (not an FDA-approved use of testosterone, by the way).[14]

Hello? Are we awake yet? My fellow sisters and brothers in Christ—this is war! We are in the midst of an unprecedented battle of ideas in our nation. A fight for freedom every bit as critical as any throughout history. You may keep your freedoms if you don't fight, but what of your children? What of your grandchildren? Will you fight for their freedoms? If not, their future is bleak.

OPPOSITION RESEARCH

In a battle, opposition research is a key component to success. One of the things coaches do to prep for the next game is watch game footage and learn their opponent's strengths and weaknesses. They study the enemy and plan accordingly.

Well, I've been watching game footage, so to speak. I have learned that the push for big government, the sexualization of our children, the erosion of parental rights, and the weakened family unit is not accidental or even a natural progression of living in an enlightened society.

It is an intentional Marxist takeover.

Karl Marx is best known for writing *The Communist Manifesto*. He believed that capitalism—free enterprise—was a system wherein the rich oppressed the poor. With an all-powerful state at the helm of the nation, Marx believed society could be directed into a classless utopia. He and his followers had no problem with shedding blood for the "greater good" of achieving this utopia.

Joseph Stalin, following Marx's blueprint, murdered between twenty million and twenty-five million innocent people. Whippings. Interrogations. Bludgeoning. Rape. The torture and raping of loved ones. Solitary confinement. Drugging. Humans were cells without a soul, according to Marxism, to be manipulated like concrete or wood or rocks for the greater good. In Marxism, there is no moral standard except that which the Party leaders make, and they're free to change it at will.

Karl Marx taught that workers should rise up against their capitalist oppressors, and faithful communists employed violence to prod the process along. However, a contingent of communists in Germany evolved into what is known as the Frankfurt School, and taught that overthrow of the capitalist regimes would come not through violent revolution, but through pioneering immorality and breaking down the family.

Under the influence of these communist scholars, "cultural Marxism" found its voice in America.

COMMUNISM EXPOSED

I was recently introduced to a book titled *The Naked Communist* written by W. Cleon Skousen, a decorated historian. The book lists forty-five communist goals for taking over the West that will blow your mind and make you beg for the days of *Leave It to Beaver* again. These forty-five Communist goals were read into the congressional record in 1963 as a warning. It is eye-opening, even much more so now than then. Following are just a few of them.[15]

> *17. Get control of the schools. Use them as transmission belts for socialism and current communist propaganda. Soften the curriculum. Get control of teachers' associations. Put the party line in textbooks.*

I was following Phyllis Schlafly back in the 1990s when she was warning about this in the schools. She exposed the danger of "outcome-based education" with its eradication of the A-B-C-D-F scoring system in favor of "pass-fail."

I saw it firsthand as an education major. Marxists conspire to change the nation by way of curriculum and policies. The teachers' union embraces an extreme leftist ideology, and they aim to win a majority by way of taxpayer-subsidized public education.

The one thing every single government program has in common is that it's run by the government; that being so, its cost continues to rise and its quality continues to drop. However, bureaucracies are insulated from criticism, and their plan to indoctrinate the nation's children has been implemented for several decades now. They have developed an undeniably powerful way to replicate their ideology.

Goal #17? Success!

19. Use student riots to foment public protests against programs or organizations which are under Communist attack.

Hmmm . . . Antifa, anyone? Student walkouts protesting gun rights? Sound familiar?

It comes as no surprise to the awakened among us that the same radical feminists who manage the "Women's March" on Washington also manage these teenagers protesting firearm freedoms. The press can't stop talking about them.

Goal #19? Success!

20. Infiltrate the press.

Conservative protests of "fake news" bias have done little to modify the media's commitment to cultural Marxism. Neither has it come anywhere near replacing them with objective news sources. And now, they're discriminating against conservative news sources, and doing it openly. They don't want competition. Facebook, YouTube, Google—they're all guilty. Censorship is the new "tolerance."

Goal #20? Incredible success!

24. Eliminate all laws governing obscenity by calling them "censorship" and a violation of free speech and free press.

The American Library Association resists any attempt to remove smut from their shelves, appealing to the right to free speech and their commitment to avoid censorship. Courts have emasculated state laws criminalizing obscenity, state legislatures have capitulated, sheriffs have backed down, and smut spreads like a poisonous disease.

Goal #24? Frightfully successful!

25. Break down cultural standards of morality by promoting pornography and obscenity in books, magazines, motion pictures, radio and TV.

Calling pornography "free speech" is all by careful design, but it doesn't hold legal muster. The U.S. Supreme Court has ruled repeatedly that the First Amendment does not protect obscene pornography. However, cowardly law enforcement and government leaders refuse to prosecute obscenity violations.

Yesterday's pornography is rated PG-13 today, and today's pornography was illegal yesterday. The slide into moral decadence knows no end. "Judge not" is their only commandment.

In Barnes & Noble bookstores and at your local county library, you can find smut everywhere, and actual nudity within reach of children. What grocery store aisle doesn't have the scantily clad cover girls of *Cosmopolitan*, with their disgusting "How to Cheat and Not Get Caught" articles in plain view of everyone?

Communism's smut mission? Success!

26. *Present homosexuality, degeneracy and promiscuity as "normal, natural, and healthy."*

Not only have we been subjected to twenty years of unrelenting "born that way" indoctrination; now we are supposed to accept as normal that biological males can actually be females. It's so bad you can't even speak against homosexuality or transgenderism in public schools or government institutions without being persecuted. Youth are encouraged to fornicate and experiment, and you are shouted down as "prudish" if you recommend abstinence.

In early 2018, a religious studies major at Indiana University in Pennsylvania got kicked out of "Christianity" class for daring to insist that, biologically, there were only two genders.[16]

The education indoctrination mission? Success!

27. *Infiltrate the churches and replace revealed religion with "social" religion. Discredit the Bible and emphasize the need for intellectual maturity which does not need a "religious crutch."*

The list of denominations and Christian leaders capitulating to the LGBT agenda, refusing to call homosexuality sin, is unfortunately growing. The number of so-called churches that march in support of homosexuality at gay pride parades is alarming. Increasing numbers of denominations are ordaining homosexuals as pastors and bishops and even holding religious services to celebrate transgender transitions and homosexual marriages.

The LGBT-church-co-opting mission? Success.

28. Eliminate prayer or any phase of religious expression in the schools on the ground that it violates the principle of "separation of church and state."

It's hard to even imagine the kind of society and public schools our forefathers created. Did you know Thomas Jefferson, the same time he coined the phrase "the wall of separation between church and state" also presided over the School District of Columbia? Can you guess what two textbooks were required in every classroom? The Holy Bible and Isaac Watts's hymnal.[17]

Can you imagine a public education system that saw its chief aim to inculcate students with Christian morality? Believe it or not, that's what our American forefathers envisioned with public education! Now our teachers can be penalized for having a Bible on their desk, or for not teaching that homosexuality is innate and involuntary.

Jefferson wrote in the Northwest Ordinance of 1787, "Religion, morality and knowledge being necessary to good government and the happiness of mankind, schools and the means of education shall forever be encouraged."

Noah Webster, our nation's first federal education bureaucrat, who has been called "the Schoolmaster of the Republic," said, "Education is useless without the Bible." The Bible was America's basic textbook in public schools for generations.

The notion that the First Amendment, which says, "Congress shall make no law respecting an establishment of religion" would give judges the right to "prohibit the free exercise thereof" in the states and penalize the proclamation of the Christian faith in public schools is absolutely absurd. Ohio is not Congress. If Ohio wants to teach Christianity is true and Islam is false in public schools at taxpayer expense, it doesn't violate the First Amendment! The denigration of our Christian heritage in public schools shows us how far the cultural Marxists have come in destroying our Christian heritage and threatening our freedoms.

Goal #28? Success.

31. *Belittle all forms of American culture and discourage the teaching of American history on the ground that it was only a minor part of "the big picture."*

When the author said to belittle all forms of American culture, he wasn't referring to what it is now but what it was then, largely guided by Christian norms.

With the much-publicized destruction of monuments to Civil War leaders in the South and the removal of George Washington's name from the titles of public schools, we are seeing the trampling of our history and of our American heritage.

Denigrating America's founders? Goal #31 fulfilled.

39. Dominate the psychiatric profession and use mental health laws as a means of gaining coercive control over those who oppose Communist goals.

It was the American Psychiatric Association who led the way removing homosexuality from the list of pathological psychosexual adaptations.[18] Even today, psychiatrists have pioneered normalizing pedophilia and encouraging sex changes in preteens and teenagers. In the name of "anti-bullying," the psychiatric profession mercilessly bullies the Christians into silence.

The mission to use psychiatry as a weapon against Christian morality? Success.

40. Discredit the family as an institution. Encourage promiscuity and easy divorce.

The family is the most important institution to propagate the Christian faith, our Christian heritage, and independent-minded critical thinking that helps keep freedom alive for the next generation. Thus, it is Enemy #1 to the cultural Marxists.

Look how far the Marxists have come! Look at how much they have accomplished. At this rate, America is headed down a perilous path of destruction if we don't turn back to our founding principles.

ROME FELL—SO CAN WE

The decline of the Roman Empire parallels in many ways the decline of the West. Militarily, Rome was still the conqueror of the world, yet the pillars that were necessary to sustain that pinnacle were crumbling. Not only was Rome inflating the value of her currency, maintaining a high level of taxation, and not assimilating immigrants, but most ominously, the family unit was disintegrating.

There was a tremendous decline of paternal authority in the home before the collapse of the empire. An overconfident and overextended military was made up of fathers who spent less and less time with their wives and children. Adultery and homosexuality became widespread, drawing the hearts of men and women away from the home into more irresponsible means of sexual gratification. Temple prostitution was common across the empire. Roman authors lamented that late in the republic, wives no longer played the ideal homemaking role they had for centuries, but women became more liberated and independent.

Divorce for any reason was increasingly frequent. All a woman had to do for a divorce was to say, "I divorce you!" three times in succession to her husband. Women did not spend time with their children and did not nurse their infants, but left them to professional nursers. Corporal punishment of children became politically incorrect, and children became increasingly drunken and sexually promiscuous. Parents came to spoil their children, resulting in irreverent and disobedient offspring who had little respect for the elderly or for social values. The Romans were masters of extreme pleasure-seeking, gambling on who would live or die in the games.

The breakdown of the family grew so widespread that Augustus, Julius Caesar's successor, tried to reverse the moral decline and restore family values by making adultery a crime and trying to force Romans into heterosexual marriage and child-rearing by establishing financial penalties for failure to do so. However, it was too little, too late.

It is easy to see how the United States of America is walking in the footsteps of Rome during her decline before her collapse. The path we travel is one intentionally and methodically paved by the cultural Marxists aiming for the decline of our republic. I have made it one of my missions to convince Americans that this is an intentional takeover by cultural Marxists, for when you know your enemy, you can defeat him. And with God's help, they can and will be defeated.

CHAPTER 10

WHY WE'VE BEEN LOSING

*We think it's un-Christlike to offend someone,
forgetting how Jesus called people "hypocrites,"
"whitewashed tombs," and "vipers!"*

The Left fights better with their weapons than we fight with ours. They use tactics that may not win popularity awards, but their tactics work. Unfortunately, far too many Christians today seem to be engaged in a battle for popularity, employing finger-in-the-wind, "consensus-building" techniques with no spiritual power. No sword of the Spirit. No cutting. No courage. For far too many comfortable American believers, the gospel simply isn't important enough to force them to inconvenience themselves or risk ridicule.

The weapons of our warfare are not carnal but mighty in God for pulling down strongholds, casting down arguments and every high thing that exalts itself against the knowledge of God, bringing every thought into captivity to the obedience of Christ, and being ready to punish all disobedience when your obedience is fulfilled. (2 Corinthians 10:4–6)

WE FEAR MAN MORE THAN
WE VALUE TRUTH

Let me illustrate. I have a friend who admitted to me that when people at work mention the Activist Mommy to him, he isn't even willing to admit he knows me, lest they disapprove of him. I mean, to not even admit you know me? My friend? He admires me, but from a distance. He doesn't want to associate with me for fear of man's disapproval. I try to let it roll off my back, but it just goes to prove how believers are more interested in being liked than in spreading truth.

"The message of the cross is foolishness to those who are perishing, but to us who are being saved it is the power of God" (1 Corinthians 1:18). There's power in the truth of God's Word. Power to heal, to save, to deliver, to restore crumbling pillars of morality in the culture. In a nation corrupted with the disease of sin, should we be afraid to mention the cure? In communities sinking in a sea of lawlessness, should we be ashamed to point people to the lifeboat?

Jesus said if we are ashamed of His words, then the Father would be ashamed of us when He returns with His mighty angels (Mark 8:38; Luke 9:26). Let it never be so!

THE LEFT UNIFIES BETTER THAN WE DO

If anyone should be able to unify, it should be believers in the Lord Jesus Christ. After all, our faith is in the King of kings and Lord of lords, Jesus Christ, the Prince of Peace.

The Left circles the wagons around their own so beautifully. They unify for the cause, regardless of all of their disagreements and differences. We couldn't unify if killer aliens were dropping from the sky to abduct our children.

From 2011 to 2017, our family worked tirelessly to help pass the Ohio Personhood Amendment—a signature-gathering ballot initiative that would have ended all abortion statewide. The wording of the amendment was something every single Bible believer and pro-life advocate could agree on. We simply defined "man" and "person" in the Ohio Constitution scientifically, to include preborn human beings. It would have protected every preborn baby in Ohio by Ohio constitutional amendment.

Yet the Catholic bishops and Ohio Right to Life and so many Christian conservative groups couldn't unify about this one thing! The excuses were as vacuous as their alternatives to banning abortion. And the blood of the children continues to soak Ohio's soil. Pathetic!

WE ARE DUPED BY
THE MANUFACTURED OUTRAGE

Most of what passes as political debate is two liberals playing a rhetorical game in front of their constituents and the press. Whether an R or a D follows their names, too often they end up doing the same thing. The liberals own both parties, and the "outrage" they have for each other in front of the public is completely manufactured. This is why you don't see my focus typically being on politics. Just look at the facts. Look at what they do.

It was the Republican governor of Massachusetts, Mitt Romney, who pioneered gay marriage in the first state in the Union, in defiance of his own legislature! It was a Republican-dominated high court that gave us not only abortion, but *Obergefell*, overruling state enforcement of the state's natural marriage laws. It was G. W. Bush that gave us the largest increase of the size of government since Lyndon Johnson's welfare expansion, with his Medicare drug entitlement nonsense. Bill Clinton tried and failed to do so because the GOP in the House had some gonads and resisted him, but a Republican president was able to pull it off!

The Republican presidents fund abortion and Planned Parenthood just as much if not more than the Democrats do! Even Trump couldn't find it within himself to disappoint the abortion lobby and funded Planned Parenthood in March 2018 to the tune of half a billion dollars! Wait—wasn't it Trump who bad-mouthed Planned Parenthood on the campaign trail and said they should be defunded, and wasn't it Hillary who promised to fund Planned Parenthood? Yep. And the Democrats hated him for it. Yet look what he's done! He went and kept Hillary's promise and broke his own. Even more, the omnibus spending bill funds Obamacare, sneaks in gun control without due process, and irresponsibly raises the budget ceiling . . . again.

The animosity the political leaders on the left and right express for each other is largely manufactured. Their followers may hate each other, but their shepherds are two wolves of the same breed. Most Republicans and Democrats squabble over inessentials and rhetoric, but they do essentially the same thing.

Why should they cater to us? After all, what are the Christians and conservatives going to do every four years? They're going to hold their noses and vote Republican because the Democrat's worse. Even if they don't like anything about the *R*, they vote *R* because that *R* will at least give us judges better than the Democrat's judges. Never mind that they keep giving us judges that perpetuate abortion and pervert marriage. Never mind that it's been a Republican majority on the High Court that gave us every godless decision pretending smut is free speech, taking prayer and the Ten Commandments out of schools, and every unconstitutional, wicked decision since 1973. Republicans can count on us every four years, no matter what they do, because the Dems are worse.

It's almost as if we fear the Democrats more than we fear God.

WE CALL VICTORY
WHAT GOD CALLS COMPROMISE

We must stop calling victory what God calls compromise. Think about abortion. The Left draws their battle line over:

- twenty-four-hour waiting periods
- the partial birth abortion ban
- dismemberment bans
- heartbeat bills that don't criminalize abortion but perpetuate *Roe v. Wade*
- defunding abortion

We fight endlessly over these nonissues, decade after decade, abortion regulation after abortion regulation, never even aiming at the target. What's the target? God's will! "It is not the will of your Father in heaven that one of these babies should perish" (Matthew 18:14, paraphrased). Not one! Yet almost every single one of our pro-life bills justifies some child killing.

"It's the best we can do," we're told. And when the judges overturn it before the ink's even dry, we hear, "Oh well. We tried. Let's get a Republican in the White House to get us some more 'strict constructionists' in the judiciary." LOL!

They take us for fools and we've played the part.

We believe the lie that true victory can't be achieved because the pushback from the Left was so loud on a small nonissue regulation bill—full of loopholes and exceptions—that there's no way we could actually pass a genuine abortion ban. So we let the enemy set the goals for us, and rest content with crumbs the judges leave behind.

Well, where should we draw the line in the sand? Hmm? How about where God does?

We can't let the Left draw the line in the sand anymore. Anything short of the abolition of all abortion is fatal compromise. We should expect just and righteous laws in this country, and nothing less. We shouldn't settle for only enforcing a little bit of our obscenity laws. No! All obscenity laws in this country should be enforced, and judges that defy the laws by rewarding those who violate the law should be impeached and prosecuted.

WE LET THE LEFT DISTRACT US
FROM FACTS WITH THEIR FEELINGS

"Why won't you let us love each other? Love is love."

That's what a gay man emailed me recently, wondering why I wouldn't support his right to marry his male lover.

Of course love is love, and you can love whoever you want. But you can't sodomize whoever you want, because your Creator, who loves you more than your own mother, forbids it. As a matter of fact, love precludes sodomy, because as 1 Corinthians 13 teaches, love "does not rejoice in iniquity, but rejoices in the truth" (v. 6). Having sex with someone of the same sex is called an abomination by God (Leviticus 18:22; 20:13), because it is so harmful. That's a fact.

Following this biblical moral standard, sodomy has been criminalized by the American states for most of American history! That's a fact. Sodomy goes hand in hand with promiscuity, disease, substance abuse, and psychological malady. (Read the facts in Dr. Paul Cameron's article, "Effect of Homosexuality upon Public Health and Social Order."[1]) Up until the Supreme Court's *Lawrence v. Texas* decision in 2003, many states had laws criminalizing sodomy, and the Supreme Court had always respected that right.

When feelings conflict with facts, we must lovingly stick with the facts.

WHEN THE GOING GETS TOUGH, WE GIVE UP

Thirty-five states ruled against gay marriage before they got Mitt Romney to give them gay marriage in 2003. Even so, the opposition to the LGBT lobby grew. By 2010, forty states had ruled against gay marriage, but the LGBT activists didn't quit. They didn't think, *Well, we should just elect more pro-gay politicians, who will give us pro-gay judges, who will give us legal gay marriage in a couple hundred years, when we finally get a majority on the Supreme Court.* Nope, they're not wimps, like the leaders of the pro-life movement. Hundreds of years of judicial precedent didn't faze the LGBT activists. They kept pushing their agenda, another state, another battlefield, another cultural boundary to break in theater and television, another ambitious legislative push against all odds.

Then, in defiance of the democratic consensus, they won *Obergefell* in 2010. But they didn't rest on their laurels. They didn't rest content with gay marriage. Immediately, they began to push the boundaries further. They went straight to the right of transgenders to use bathrooms and locker rooms of the opposite sex.

It doesn't matter how unpopular their idea is. They. Never. Give. Up.

When in 2001 and 2005, the Supreme Court ruled that states may not violate federal policy when it came to medical marijuana, what did the Left do? Were they, like, "Oh, well. We've got to elect more pro-pot presidents, who will give us pro-pot judges so that one day many decades from now we could get that pro-pot majority"? No, they pushed their agenda and urged state defiance of federal policy. And now more than half the states in the nation have legal medical and/or recreational marijuana, in defiance of the federal government.

I sure wish National Right to Life would love their preborn neighbor as much as the pot smokers love their pot!

I'm sick of losing our kids, our families, our prosperity, our protections, our Christian heritage, and our religious liberty to these godless, hedonistic thugs. Can we have at least as much ambition for God as they have for godlessness?

WE THINK THE SECOND COMING OF JESUS
IS AN EXCUSE FOR APATHY

"Jesus is coming back in my lifetime, and the world is just going to get worse until that happens. So why fight it?"

It is so sad that Jesus's coming has been a motive for withdrawal from the battle and passivity and compromise on the battle line. Jesus may come in our lifetime, but He may not. To appeal to the Second Coming to justify letting Satan devour the souls of our children in abortion clinics and in public schools, to trample our Constitution and our Christian heritage, and to pervert the holy institution of marriage—what a blasphemy!

As I alluded to earlier, in one of my favorite parables about the second coming of Christ, the Master orders the servants to "occupy till I come" (Luke 19:13 KJV). To occupy something is not to merely fill up space, but to possess it.

God wants His servants to "occupy" this land with righteous laws and judgments, with truth, with the honor of God's law and majesty. Not to hide behind our stained-glass fortresses while the devil conquers hard-fought land, perverts the truth, and tramples the law of God. This is a grievous shame to the body of Christ.

The Second Coming should be a motive to act, to conquer, to do justice for the preborn and secure righteous laws. Hurry, quick, before Jesus comes back! After all, what happened to the "unprofit-able servant" who buried his talent, who did not profit his master? He was "cast . . . into the outer darkness," where there is "weeping and gnashing of teeth." (Read about it in Matthew 25.)

If you continue to give way to the devil's militant rage against all that is good and holy in our nation, if you continue to refuse to implement righteous laws and judgments in the place of law-lessness, and if you fail to secure freedom for posterity, the day of Christ's coming may not be a delight to you at all, but a terror.

WE THINK PRAYER REPLACES ACTION

Prayer is powerful! In Luke 10:2, Jesus told His disciples to pray for laborers to go into His harvest, but in the very next verse, He sent them out, and verse 1 tells us He sent them two by two. Jesus prayed in the Garden of Gethsemane, but that wasn't enough. He had to go to the cross and die for you and me. He sacrificed. He agonized. He was despised and rejected for us. He bled. And ultimately, He died for you and me. He didn't just pray and stop there.

If you put yourself on the battle line of this culture to trample evil and win victories, you'd better be prepared to fight. It's going to start with prayer, for sure, but if it ends with prayer, then you've fought its answer, because God wants to use us to answer it.

If you aren't willing to be feet to your prayers, then don't pray. Repent.

WE ATTEMPT TO BE "NICER THAN JESUS"

We think it's un-Christlike to offend someone, forgetting how Jesus called people "hypocrites," "whitewashed tombs," and "vipers!" (Matthew 12:34; 15:7; 16:3; 22:18; 23:13, 27, 33, et al.) He over-turned the tables of those who sold in the temple, lashing his whip at them. This took place, according to the Bible, in the first and third years of His ministry. Who knows? It may have been an annual event for Jesus and His disciples.

If you want to fight for America to not go the way of Rome and be sacked by foreign invaders, you're going to need some fire in your gut. If you want to fight for the end of abortion, it's going to take some courage.

"Who will rise up for me against the evildoers?" we read in Psalm 94:16. "Who will stand [with] me against the workers of iniquity?"

I will. Will you?

WE THINK WE HAVE TO BUILD
A CONSENSUS TO SUCCEED

No, we don't. Stop trying to play politics, dulling the two-edged sword to creep your way to that ever-elusive majority. That's not the kind of leadership God's looking for. Did David try to get some soldiers together to get a majority over the Philistines before he ran toward Goliath? Do the math: 1 man + God = majority. When David obeyed God, his "mighty men" followed him (see 2 Samuel 10). They sought God out. They were still a minority, but God did the drawing and the empowering.

Even if you did have a majority, God would send away most of your troops so that He alone could get the glory. He did it before, when Israel had superior numbers preparing to conquer the Midianites. God whittled down their superior advantage and sent most of the troops home from the battle until they were underdogs (see Judges 7).

Samuel Adams is believed to have said, "It does not take a majority to prevail, but rather an irate, tireless minority keen to set brush fires of freedom in the minds of men." We must be that irate, tireless minority, Activist Mommies and Daddies! With God, all things are possible!

Martin Luther King Jr. once said, "Human progress is neither automatic nor inevitable. . . . Every step towards the goal of justice requires sacrifice, suffering, and struggle; the tireless exertions and passionate concern of dedicated individuals."[2]

Are you down for the struggle? Then pray. Are you praying for victory? Then struggle. Get in the battle. Make a move for God. God has won the victory, but it is up to us to enforce it—to "occupy" till He returns.

Your action puts God on the spot. See if He won't rise to the occasion and move on your behalf!

CHAPTER 11

HOW WE WILL WIN

Winning the battle for our culture isn't a fight to eradicate sinners, but to fight the normalization and acceptance of evil.

One of the wisest men who ever lived once said, "Righteousness exalts a nation, but sin is a reproach to a people" (Proverbs 14:34). Sin is a reproach. It makes us personally weak as individuals and it makes our culture weak and susceptible to be mastered. We will always have sinners with us. We will always have to resist evil and be the moral conscience of culture. Winning the battle for our culture isn't a fight to eradicate sinners but to fight the normalization and acceptance of evil.

WHAT IS OUR PROBLEM?

This fight is a problem that can't be fixed by voting Republican or building a wall. Remember: "*righteousness* exalts a nation, but sin is a reproach to any people" (Proverbs 14:34, emphasis mine). Alexis de Tocqueville said it so perfectly: "America is great because she is good. If America ceases to be good, America will cease to be great."[1] All the monetary and military success in the world will never make us good if we continue to turn our backs against the Divine Lawgiver. We desperately need a spiritual turnaround in this nation. Ultimately, our struggle is spiritual, and the battle we fight is between good and evil.

BEING SALTY AND LIT

In order for us to win the spiritual battle between light and darkness, so that our nation is good again, we the people must be salt and light again, or as I like to say, salty and lit. If any of you have teenagers, you've heard the terms "salty" and "lit" a thousand more times than you wish you had. If teenagers like something or think it's cool, they say "LIT!" If someone's upset about something, they say, "Why so salty?" or in other words, "Why are you so upset?"

As you may know, the Activist Mommy is known for being "salty" about the agenda to destroy the moral fabric of our nation and pervert the minds of our children. That's why I recorded a video of myself burning a copy of *Teen Vogue* magazine. That's why I exposed Facebook's bias toward Christians with a worldwide media story that resulted in an apology from Facebook. That's why I sparked a global movement of outraged parents called "Sex Ed Sit Out," which resulted in major press events in eleven cities and three countries on the same day across the world.

Jesus said, "You are the salt of the earth; but if the salt loses its flavor, how shall it be seasoned? It is then good for nothing but to be thrown out and trampled underfoot by men" (Matthew 5:13).

History reveals that being "trampled underfoot by men" is not metaphorical. In times of great apathy and sin in the church, judgment comes. In the book of Revelation chapters 2 and 3, read God's warnings to the seven churches! Bitter, horrible judgment was prophesied to God's people if they did not repent of their sin and live for Christ. Prison, defeat, and death.

Some don't agree with my methodology and think I'm too confrontational, but I have to ask, what are they accomplishing? Just as saltiness is sometimes required for food to be preserved, saltiness is also required for our nation to be preserved.

WHAT IS LOVE, REALLY?

God is love, and we are to model love as well. But love looks very different depending on the situation. For instance, if I am approached by a woman contemplating abortion or a homosexual who has sincere questions, love looks like chapter 7 of this book. Love is patient and kind. But if you dramatically change the situation, and I am being approached by a pedophile who wants to molest my child, love looks like the death penalty. Can I get an amen? Sometimes people fail to see that I am not just reaching individuals—I am also fighting godless movements that are aggressively attacking our God-given rights and our children's innocence. The approach cannot always be the same. When Jesus spoke to the woman at the well, He told her of the living water she could receive (John 4), but when He got righteously indignant about the corruption in God's house, He started turning over tables (Mark 11:15–17). Some situations call for confrontation. Jesus was definitely more confrontational than I am!

It took aggressive confrontation for me to get a pedophile public service announcement ad removed from a radio station in Arizona. We confronted the radio station owner about playing this dangerous ad that taught men how to hide their child porn from police detection. He doubled down and committed to keep running the ad, so we started publicly calling out and humiliating the radio station owner, and ultimately had to call the local sheriff. We were victorious, and the ad was finally removed. More nice conversations with the radio station owner might have appeared more loving, but it would not have actually been more loving, because it wouldn't have worked. It took an aggressive approach to protect innocent children. Love protects the innocent, even if we look angry in the process.

TOUGHEN UP OR SHUT UP

American Christians need to toughen up and "grow some chest hair" if we are ever going to take back our culture from the social Marxists who are hell-bent on destroying everything good. Marxists have intentionally, through the feminist movement, softened and feminized America. Don't fall for it. We women don't want you men to be sissies. You're being lied to by the American media, the entertainment industry, and the educational elite. They represent a very small but loud fraction of the population. When are we going to get louder and bolder than them? They fight for perversion. We fight for righteousness. Who should be more courageous? As Scripture teaches, "The wicked flee when no one pursues, but the righteous are bold as a lion" (Proverbs 28:1). We are the ones with the cause worth fighting for, but we must wake up to the fact that anything worth having takes effort and energy to preserve and protect.

It took publicly burning a *Teen Vogue* magazine and an aggressive campaign of calling their advertisers with boycott threats for us to see the printed magazine closed down. It took weeks of angry media interviews, confrontational tweets to the author and the digital editorial director, and weeks of outraged phone calls to advertisers. We brought down an industry giant, not by merely praying prayers or attending church, but by being salt and light in our culture.

Salt sometimes stings, and light can burn the eyes. What salt and light looks like greatly depends on the setting. The Jesus who will cast sinners into hell is just as loving as the Jesus who chose to be crucified and prayed, "Father, forgive them" (Luke 23:34). Different circumstances call for different measures. Be careful to not be overly critical of someone who doesn't appear as loving as you feel he or she should. You just might be nicer than Jesus wants you to be.

We mama bears didn't look too loving when we were trolling the City of Westerville (OH) on Facebook and Twitter for issuing permits to a shady Asian massage parlor, which was actually a sex brothel set up next to a high school to get the young men to buy their massage and sex services. When I thought about those boys being intentionally targeted by that brothel across the street, and I heard the lame excuses the city was giving for issuing their permits, I think lava actually squirted out of my eyes, or my ears, or both. I was angry, and the City of Westerville got ten earfuls from me! Guess what? The police raided the store and the storeowner's home. The owner is in trouble with the law and won't be doing business in Westerville—that's for sure![2] My tongue may have been sharp on Twitter, but that was the most loving thing I could have done for those targeted high school boys and those girls being sex trafficked. We were salt and light, and we prevailed.

WE HAVE DROPPED THE BALL

Let me ask you a question. If we were really being salt and light the last decade as we are commanded to be, would drag queens be reading stories to our kids in public libraries? Would our daughters be forced to share a locker room with boys? Would more than three thousand babies be murdered every day through abortion? Would public schools be teaching our kids—at taxpayer expense—how to have anal and oral sex and masturbate each other? No! This nation stinks with rottenness because we, the salt, have lost our saltiness. Shame on us.

Let's face it. We want to be liked. We want to be highly esteemed among others. Who doesn't? This desire for acceptance comes with a temptation to always "go along to get along." But if we lose our saltiness, Jesus said we would be trampled underfoot by men. And that's precisely what we are seeing. We are being trampled by rogue leftist judges on the courts, by social media giants who stifle the voices of Americans, and by a massive federal bureaucracy that forces us to pay for many things we find unconscionable.

Perhaps you're familiar with the following quotation: "If I profess with loudest voice and clearest exposition every portion of the truth of God except that little point which the world and the devil are at that moment attacking, I am not confessing Christ, however boldly I may be professing Christ. Where the battle rages, there the loyalty of the soldier is proved, and to be steady on all the battlefield besides, is mere flight and disgrace if he flinches at that point."[3]

Let me tell you "where the battle rages" in America today. In the bloody hallways of America's abortion facilities, in America's public school indoctrination camps, and in the court chambers of America's judicial tyrants. If we attend church and mind our own business but fail to address and influence these various battlefields where Satan is gaining ground, we will lose. If we will engage and trust God with our efforts, there will be no end to the miracles we will see as God gives us victory after victory.

If you are tired of your values being trampled, then you must get out of the saltshaker. You must get out of your home and the four walls of the church and impact your culture. We must be willing to sting the wounds of our culture with the application of God's salty message. That means you're not going to always be popular and some people are going to get offended. But listen: salt doesn't sting when you place it on healthy flesh. Salt stings when there is an open wound.

Our nation suffers from an open wound called sin, and God wants to use us to bring healing. May a movement of salty men and women shake off the fear of man and arise to the great task of preserving our nation and rescuing future generations.

NOTES

INTRODUCTION

1   World Health Organization (WHO), cited in Worldometers, accessed September 14, 2018, http://www.worldometers.info/abortions/.

2   Megan Fox, "Demonic Clown Drag Queen Does Story Time at Michelle Obama Public Library," PJ Media, October 17, 2017, https://pjmedia.com/parenting/demonic-clown-drag-queen-story-time-michelle-obama-public-library/.

3   Carol Brown, "Public School Teaches the Shahada, the Islamic Prayer for Conversions," *American Thinker* (blog), February 12, 2015, https://www.americanthinker.com/blog/2015/02/public_school_teaches_the_shahada_the_islamic_prayer_for_conversions.html.

4   Exodus 1; Daniel 3; 6; Acts 4:13–20.

5   Joshua Gill, "Satanists Tell Supporters to Force Christian Bakers to 'Make a Cake for Satan,'" *Daily Caller*, September 28, 2017, http://dailycaller.com/2017/09/28/satanists-tell-supporters-to-force-christian-bakers-to-make-same-sex-wedding-cakes/.

6   Charlotte Santry, "All Schools Should Adopt Gender-Neutral Uniforms, Say Lib-Dems," *Tes*, February 28, 2018, https://www.tes.com/news/all-schools-should-adopt-gender-neutral-uniforms-say-lib-dems.

7   Emily Jones, "'It is Disappointing': Praying Football Coach Faces Another Loss," CBN News, January 25, 2018, http://www1.cbn.com/cbnnews/us/2018/january/it-is-disappointing-praying-football-coach-faces-another-loss.

8   Mark Hodges, "Boston City Hall Denies Christian Flag, but Allows LGBT Flags," LifeSiteNews, September 21, 2017, https://www.lifesitenews.com/news/boston-bans-christian-groups-flag-allows-transgender-flag.

9   Paul Bois, "A Nobel Peace Prize for . . . Planned Parenthood?!," Daily Wire, September 19, 2017, https://www.dailywire.com/news/21261 /planned-parenthood-nobel-prize-paul-bois.

10 Wade Trimmer, "Too Many Shirkers!," Grace Fellowship of Augusta, October 12, 2017, http://www.gracefellowshipofaugusta.com/pastor -wades-blog/post/too-many-shirkers.

11 Avery Foley, "Canada Forces Government Speech and Bans Bible Verses," Answers in Genesis, August 6, 2017, https:// answersingenesis.org/religious-freedom/canada-forces-government -speech-and-bans-bible-verses/.

CHAPTER 1

1   "Attorney: Kim Davis Had to Change Phone Number Because of Death Threats," Fox News Insider, September 14, 2015, http://insider .foxnews.com/2015/09/14/attorney-mat-staver-kim-davis-receiving -death-threats-had-change-phone-number.

2   Alan Blinder and Richard Pérez-Peña, "Kentucky Clerk Denies Same-Sex Marriage Licenses, Defying Court," New York Times, September 1, 2015, https://www.nytimes.com/2015/09/02/us/same -sex-marriage-kentucky-kim-davis.html.

3   Ky. Const. § 233A.

4   David Sivak, "Fact Check: Have There Been 60 Million Abortions since Roe v. Wade?," Check Your Fact, July 3, 2018, http:// checkyourfact.com/2018/07/03/fact-check-60-million-abortions/.

CHAPTER 2

1   "Part to the Target Officials Ask Us to Leave," YouTube video, 2:51, Coach Dave Daubenmire challenging Target's bathroom policy, posted by CoachDave.TV, April 26, 2016, https://www.youtube.com /watch?v=bLQ2kuWqQew.

2   " VIDEO: Coach Dave Daubenmire Confirms Men Can Enter Women's Restrooms at All Target Stores Nationwide," Americans for Truth about Homosexuality, May 1, 2016, https://americansfortruth. com/2016/05/01/video-coach-dave-daubenmire-confirms-men-can -enter-womens-restroom-at-all-target-stores/.

3   AFA, "An Update from AFA President, Tim Wildmon," Sign the Boycott Target Pledge!, accessed September 14, 2018, https://afa.net /target.

4   Jen Retallick/Hamilton Strategies, "Target CEO Admits Bathroom Policy Announcement Was Huge Mistake," *Charisma News*, April 6, 2017, https://www.charismanews.com/us/64114-target-ceo-admits -bathroom-policy-announcement-was-huge-mistake.

5   "U.S. Departments of Justice and Education Release Joint Guidance to Help Schools Ensure the Civil Rights of Transgender Students," news release, United States Department of Justice, May 13, 2016, https://www.justice.gov/opa/pr/us-departments-justice-and -education-release-joint-guidance-help-schools-ensure-civil-rights.

6   Warner Todd Huston, "Target Sales Drop amid Transgender Promotion, Consumer Boycott, $10 Billion Stock Crash," Breitbart, May 19, 2016, https://www.breitbart.com/big-government/2016/05 /19/target-earnings-drop-protests-rise/; and Vivek Saxena, "1 Year after Trans Bathroom Move, Target Has Lost $10 Billion in Value," *Western Journal Conservative Tribune*, February 10, 2017, https:// www.westernjournal.com/ct/year-after-bathroom-move-target/.

7   Tyler O'Neil, "Johns Hopkins Research: No Evidence People Are Born Gay or Transgender," PJ Media, August 23, 2016, https:// pjmedia.com/trending/2016/08/23/johns-hopkins-research-no -evidence-people-are-born-gay-or-transgender/; Lawrence S. Mayer and Paul R. McHugh, *New Atlantis* 50, *Special Report: Sexuality and Gender* (Fall 2016).

8   Claire Chretien, "Bathrooms Are Just the Beginning: A Scary Look into the Trans Movement's End Goals," LifeSite News, May 6, 2016, https://www.lifesitenews.com/news/bathrooms-are-just-the -beginning-a-scary-look-into-the-trans-movements-end. Chretien's article is referring to an article Wilchins wrote for the *Advocate*, titled "We'll Win the Bathroom Battle When the Binary Burns," April 29, 2016, available at https://www.advocate.com/commentary/2016/4/29 /well-win-bathroom-battle-when-binary-burns.

9   Wilchins, "We'll Win the Bathroom Battle When the Binary Burns."

10 "2015 U.S. Trangender Survey—Executive Summary," National

Center for Transgender Equality, December 2016, https://
transequality.org/sites/default/files/docs/usts/USTS-Executive
-Summary-Dec17.pdf.

11 Paul McHugh, "Transgender Surgery Isn't the Solution," *Wall Street
Journal*, June 12, 2014 (updated May 13, 2016), https://www.wsj.com
/articles/paul-mchugh-transgender-surgery-isnt-the-solution
-1402615120.

12 For instance, see Jennifer Bilek, "Who Are the Rich, White Men
Institutionalizing Transgender Ideology?," The Federalist, February
20, 2018, http://thefederalist.com/2018/02/20/rich-white-men
-institutionalizing-transgender-ideology/.

13 Greg Abbott (@GregAbbott_TX), "I announced today that Texas
is fighting this. Obama can't rewrite the Civil Rights Act. He's not
a King," Twitter, May 12, 2016, 8:48 p.m., https://twitter.com
/GregAbbott_TX/status/730968042281144320.

14 Adapted from Merrill Hope, "'We Will Not Yield to Blackmail,' Says
Texas Lt. Gov. on Transgender Bathrooms," Breitbart, May 13, 2016,
https://www.breitbart.com/texas/2016/05/13/will-not-yield
-blackmail-says-texas-lt-gov-transgender-bathroom.

15 Gov. Asa Hutchinson (@AsaHutchinson), Twitter post, May 13,
2016, quoted in "BREAKING: 12 States Stand Up Against Obama's
Unlawful Trans Bathroom Decree," Top Right News, March 14,
2016, http://toprightnews.com/breaking-12-states-stand-up-against
-obamas-unlawful-trans-bathroom-decree/.

16 Governor Matt Bevin, "In response to President Obama's proposed
bathroom rules for public schools . . . ," Facebook, May 13, 2016,
https://www.facebook.com/GovMattBevin/posts/1557197601246794.

17 Kiley Crossland/WORLD, "Parents Lose Custody of Transgender
Teen," Baptist Press, February 20, 2018, http://www.bpnews.net
/50398/parents-lose-custody-of-transgender-teen.

18 Steve Straub, "Rebellion to Tyrants Is Obedience to God, Benjamin
Franklin," FederalistPapers.org, November 30, 2012, https://
thefederalistpapers.org/founders/franklin/rebellion-to-tyrants
-is-obedience-to-god-benjamin-franklin.

19 Martin Luther King Jr., from a sermon preached in Selma, Alabama, March 8, 1965, quoted in Tracy Lee, "MLK Jr. Quotes: Seven Powerful Sayings on 50th Anniversary of Assassination," *Newsweek*, April 4, 2018, https://www.newsweek.com/martin-luther-king-jr-50 -years-after-assassination-here-are-his-inspirational-870297.

20 Michelle Cretella, MD, "Gender Dysphoria in Children," Gender Dysphoria in Children, June 2017, https://www.acpeds.org/the -college-speaks/position-statements/gender-dysphoria-in-children.

CHAPTER 3

1 "What Ladies Everywhere Want to Say to the Women's Marchers!!," YouTube video, 3:32, posted by "The Activist Mommy," January 27, https://www.youtube.com/watch?v=3fW5Ee4Of1g.

2 Kirk Copple, "If Every Person on Earth Was to Be Given an Equal Portion of Inhabitable Land, How Much Land Would Each Person Get?," Quora, February 12, 2016, https://www.quora.com/If-every -person-on-earth-was-to-be-given-an-equal-portion-of-inhabitable -land-how-much-land-would-each-person-get.

3 Max Roser, "Fertility Rate," Our World in Data, https:// ourworldindata.org/fertility-rate (first published in 2014; substantive revision published on December 2, 2017).

4 Carol Hardy Vincent, Laura A. Hanson, and Carla N. Argueta, Federal *Land Ownership: Overview and Data* (Congressional Research Service), 1, https://fas.org/sgp/crs/misc/R42346.pdf.

5 "Total Fertility Rate," World Health Organization, http://www.searo .who.int/entity/health_situation_trends/data/chi/TFR/en/.

6 Associated Press, "U.S. Births Hit a 30-Year Low," CBS News, May 17, 2018, http://www.searo.who.int/entity/health_situation_trends/data /chi/TFR/en/.

7 Pew, "The Future of World Religions: Population Growth Projections, 2010–2050," Pew Research Center, April 2, 2015, http://www .pewforum.org/2015/04/02/religious-projections-2010-2050/.

8 Yusuf Ali translation, http://corpus.quran.com/translation .jsp?chapter=9&verse=5.

9 Emily Foxhall, "Complaint: Katy-Area Teacher Fired for Refusing to
   Address girl, 6, as Transgender Boy," *Houston Chronicle*, November
   10, 2015, https://www.houstonchronicle.com/neighborhood/katy
   /news/article/Complaint-Katy-area-teacher-fired-for-refusing
   -6623487.php; Brianna Heldt, "Indiana Teacher Forced to Resign over
   Refusal to Use Trangender Pronouns," Townhall, June 6, 2018, https://
   townhall.com/tipsheet/briannaheldt/2018/06/06/indiana-teacher
   -forced-to-resign-over-refusal-to-use-transgender-pronouns
   -n2487919; Eugenie Scott, "Minnesota Teacher Sues District over
   Evolution," Reports of the *National Center for Science Education* 19,
   no. 6 (Fall 1999), 8–9, https://ncse.com/library-resource
   /minnesota-teacher-sues-district-over-evolution.
10 Travis Rieder, "Science proves kids are bad for Earth. Morality
   suggests we stop having them," *Think* (NBC blog), November 15, 2017.
11 Margaret Sanger, *Woman Rebel* vol. 1, no. 1, reprinted in Sanger,
   Woman and the New Race (New York: Brentanos, 1922) ,p 61.
12 Sanger, *Woman Rebel*.
13 Margaret Sanger, *The Pivot of Civilization* (New York: Brentanos,
   1922), 116–17, 187.
14 Margaret Sanger, letter to Dr. Clarence Gamble, 255 Adams Street,
   Milton, MA, December 19, 1939 (the Sophia Smith Collection, Smith
   College, North Hampton, MA), discussed in Linda Gordon, *Woman's
   Body, Woman's Right: A Social History of Birth Control in America*
   (New York: Grossman, 1976).
15 Videos in "Hillary Clinton Said She 'Admires' Margaret Sanger-
   Truth!," TruthorFiction.com, June 10, 2015, in which Clinton can be
   seen and heard making this statement.
16 "Women's March Organizer Linda Sarsour Supports Sharia Law-
   MostlyTruth!," TruthorFiction.com, January 24, 2017, https://www
   .truthorfiction.com/womens-march-organizer-linda-sarsour
   -supports-sharia-law-reported/.
17 Glenn Kessler, "Here Are the Facts Behind That '79 cent' Pay Gap
   Factoid," *Washington Post*, " April 14, 2016, https://www
   .washingtonpost.com/news/fact-checker/wp/2016/04/14/here

-are-the-facts-behind-that-79-cent-pay-gap-factoid/?utm_term=
.dd7dcb470682.

CHAPTER 4

1 Embedded video in Joe Schaeffer, "Abortion Provider: We Should
   Admit 'It's Violence, It's a Person, It's Killing,'" NewsMax, November
   2, 2015, Tellingly, the once-embedded video containing this
   statement is no longer available on many conservative sites that
   once included it. It "has been removed for violating YouTube's
   Terms of Service."
2 Schaeffer, "Abortion Provider."
3 Text and video at Alexandra Desanctis, "'I Might . . . Pull Off
   a Leg or Two,'" *National Review*, May 25, 2017, https://www
   .nationalreview.com/2017/05/undercover-video-center-medical
   -progress-exposes-gruesome-abortion-practices/.
4 Desanctis, "I Might . . . Pull Off a Leg or Two."
5 Steven Ertelt, "57,762,169 Abortions in America Since Roe vs. Wade
   in 1973," LifeNews.com, January 21, 2015, https://www.lifenews.com
   /2015/01/21/57762169-abortions-in-america-since-roe-vs-wade
   -in-1973/.
6 ACLJ.org, "A Balance Sheet of Death: Planned Parenthood's Abortion
   Business Profits Continue to Soar as Prenatal and Miscarriage
   "Services" Precipitously Dwindle," ACLJ, January 2018, https://aclj
   .org/pro-life/a-balance-sheet-of-death-planned-parenthoods-
   abortion-business-profits-continue-to-soar-as-prenatal-and
   -miscarriage-services-precipitously-dwindle.
7 Dr. Susan Berry, "Watch: Planned Parenthood's Myth That Abortion
   Represents Only 3 Percent of Its Services," Breitbart, September 14,
   2016, https://www.breitbart.com/big-government/2016/09/14
   /watch-planned-parenthoods-myth-abortion-represents-3-percent
   -services/.

CHAPTER 6

1 Saul Alinsky, *Rules for Radicals* (New York: Vintage Books, 1971), 128.

2 https://www.facebook.com/theactivistmommy/
posts/1540661532718657.

3 Emily Hanford, "Angela Duckworth and the Research on 'Grit,'"
American Public Media, accessed September 18, 2018, http://
americanradioworks.publicradio.org/features/tomorrows-college
/grit/angela-duckworth-grit.html; Jonah Lehrer, "Which Traits
Predict Success? (The Importance of Grit)," *Wired*, March 14, 2011,
https://www.wired.com/2011/03/what-is-success-true-grit/.

4 "Hell Week," NavySEALS.com, accessed September 18, 2018, https://
navyseals.com/nsw/hell-week-0/.

CHAPTER 8

1 Gigi Engle: "A GUIDE TO ANAL SEX: Anal Sex: What You Need to
Know: How to Do It the RIGHT Way," *Teen Vogue*, May 16,
2018, https://www.teenvogue.com/story/anal-sex-what-you-need
-to-know.

2 Celia Hooper, "Surgeon General Advises Doctors to Teach Patients
About Condoms," United Press International, October 13, 1987,
https://www.upi.com/Archives/1987/10/13/Surgeon-general-advises
-doctors-to-teach-patients-about-condoms/5449561096000/.

3 Lianne Laurence, "Ontario's Dangerous Sex-Ed Is Indoctrination
Not Science Says U.S. Psychiatrist to Large Audience," LifeSiteNews,
August 20, 2015, https://www.lifesitenews.com/news/ontarios
-dangerous-sex-ed-is-indoctrination-not-science-says-u.s.-psychiatr.

4 "Anal Sex and HIV Risk," Centers for Disease Control and
Prevention (last updated October 27, 2016), https://www.cdc.gov
/hiv/risk/analsex.html.

5 You can view this video (posted July 13, 2017) on my Facebook page,
at https://www.facebook.com/theactivistmommy/videos
/1344469902338122/.

6 Charlene Aaron, "Activist Mommy Starts 'Operation Pull Teen
Vogue' after Mag Peddles Perversion to Minors," CBN News, July 17,
2017, http://www1.cbn.com/cbnnews/us/2017/july/activist-mommy
-starts-operation-pull-teen-vogue-after-mag-peddles-sexual
-perversion-to-minors.

7   Stoyan Zaimov, *Christian Post*, July 18, 2017, https://www.
    christianpost.com/news/activist-mommy-teen-vogues-sex-guide
    -crime-texted-minors-192377/.

8   Hemant Mehta, *Friendly Atheist* (blog), Patheos, July 17, 2017, http://
    friendlyatheist.patheos.com/2017/07/17/activist-mommy-claims
    -teen-vogue-broke-the-law-with-its-anal-sex-article/.

9   Todd Starnes, *Todd's American Dispatch*, Fox News, July 18, 2017,
    http://www.foxnews.com/opinion/2017/07/18/teen-vogue-defends
    -teaching-kids-how-to-engage-in-sodomy.html.

10 Joe Marusak, "Franklin Graham Blasts Teen Vogue as a 'Porn
    Magazine,'" *Charlotte Observer,* July 20, 2017, https://www
    .charlotteobserver.com/news/local/article162817473.html.

11 See Aaron, "Activist Mommy Starts 'Operation Pull Teen Vogue'
    after Mag Peddles Perversion to Minors."

12 18 U.S.C. § 1470: Transfer of obscene material to minors. See
    Citizen's Guide to U.S. Federal Law on Obscenity, United States
    Department of Justice, https://www.justice.gov/criminal-ceos
    /citizens-guide-us-federal-law-obscenity.

13 Phillip Picardi (@pfpicardi), "The backlash to this article is rooted in
    homophobia . . . ," Twitter, July 14, 2017, 11:05 a.m., https://twitter
    .com/pfpicardi/status/885923251624574977.

14 See Melanie Mignucci, "Back to School Awards 2017: The Best
    Health and Wellness Products." *Teen Vogue*, https://www.teenvogue.
    com/gallery/back-to-school-awards-2017-health-wellness-products/;
    Claire Chretien, "Teen Vogue Recommends Vibrators on Back to
    School List," LifeSiteNews, August 22, 2017, https://www.lifesitenews
    .com/news/teen-vogues-back-to-school-list-includes-vibrators.

15 Alexandra Steigrad, "Condé Nast to Cease Teen Vogue in Print, Cut
    80 Jobs and Lower Mag Frequencies," WWD, November 2, 2017,
    https://wwd.com/business-news/media/conde-nast-to-close-teen
    -vogue-cut-80-jobs-and-lower-mag-frequencies-11040148/.

16 Samuel Smith, "'Activist Mommy' Hails Victory After Condé Nast
    Halts Teen Vogue Print Edition, *CP* U.S., November 3, 2017, https://
    www.christianpost.com/news/activist-mommy-hails-victory-after
    -conde-nast-halts-teen-vogue-print-edition-205348/.

17 "Whitney Young High School Pulls Plug on 'Troubling' Sex Ed Programs After Lawsuit Filed by Parents," *Cook County Record,* April 19, 2018, https://cookcountyrecord.com/stories/511395542-whitney -young-high-school-pulls-plug-on-troubling-sex-ed-programs-after -lawsuit-filed-by-parents; also see *Wagenmaker vs. Kenner* complaint in the Circuit Court of Cook County, Illinois, filed April 16, 2018, https://www.thomasmoresociety.org/wp-content/uploads/2018 /04/COUR.Complaint.EmergencyInjunctive.Relief.2018-04-16 .FILED_.pdf.

CHAPTER 9

1 Juvenal, quoted in "Bread and Circuses and Other Things," *Life* magazine, February 28, 1938, 41.

2 Matthew J. Brouillette, "Study: Conclusion: Restoring a Free Market in Education," Mackinac Center for Public Policy, January 9, 2001, https://www.mackinac.org/3243.

3 Ali Meyer, "Americans Must Work Jan. 1 Through April 24 Just to Pay Taxes," cnsnews.com, March 31, 2015, https://www.cnsnews .com/news/article/ali-meyer/americans-must-work-jan-1-through -april-24-just-pay-taxes.

4 Samuel B. Casey, JD, in Con 3, "Should Abortion Be Legal?," ProCon .org, last updated May 16, 2017, https://abortion.procon.org/view .answers.php?questionID=001447#answer-id-014189.

5 Tyjen Tsai and Paola Scommegna, "U.S. Has World's Highest Incarceration Rate," PRB (Population Reference Bureau), August 10, 2012, https://www.prb.org/us-incarceration/.

6 Veronique de Rugy and Justin Leventhal, "Per Capita Federal Spending Continues to Grow," Mercatus Center (George Mason University), February 12, 2018, https://www.mercatus.org /publications/per-capita-federal-spending-growth.

7 U.S.DebtClock.org, accessed September 19, 2018, http://www .usdebtclock.org/.

8 Michael Lombardi, MBA, "Why the U.S. Dollar Is Crashing in Value," *Lombardi Letter*, September 15, 2017, https://www.lombardiletter

.com/u-s-dollar-crashing-value/17502/, citing "The Daily History of the Debt Results," TreasuryDirect, as of September 7, 2017, https://treasurydirect.gov/NP/debt/search?startMonth=09&startDay=07&startYear=2017&endMonth=&endDay=&endYear=.

9 "Average Salaries for Americans—Median Salaries for Common Jobs," Fox Business, July 9, 2015, https://www.foxbusiness.com/features/average-salaries-for-americans-median-salaries-for-common-jobs.

10 Merrill Matthews, "We've Crossed the Tipping Point; Most Americans Now Receive Government Benefits," *Forbes*, July 2, 2014, https://www.forbes.com/sites/merrillmatthews/2014/07/02/weve-crossed-the-tipping-point-most-americans-now-receive-government-benefits/#33a19e523e6c.

11 "Congress and the New Deal: Social Security," citing President Roosevelt in 1941, https://www.archives.gov/exhibits/treasures_of_congress/text/page19_text.html, accessed September 19, 2018/.

12 See Sarah Taylor, "Delaware gender policy would allow students to change identity in schools without parent permission," TheBlaze, November 9, 2017, https://www.theblaze.com/news/2017/11/09/delaware-gender-policy-would-allow-students-to-change-identity-in-schools-without-parent-permission.

13 See Brandon Morse, "'TransKids' Site Sells Prosthetic Penises For 'Trans' Little Girls to Wear," RedState, December 28, 2017, https://www.redstate.com/brandon_morse/2017/12/28/transkids-site-sells-prosthetic-penises-little-girls-wear/.

14 See Nicole Russell, "Ohio Judge Strips Custody From Parents For Not Letting Daughter Take Trans Hormones," The Federalist, February 20, 2018, http://thefederalist.com/2018/02/20/ohio-judge-strips-custody-parents-not-letting-daughter-taking-trans-hormones/.

15 W. Cleon Skousen, "Current Communist Goals," in *The Naked Communist* (Salt Lake City: Izzard Ink, 1958, 2017), 269–72.

16 Caleb Parke, "College Student Kicked Out of Class for Telling Professor There Are Only Two Genders," Fox News Channel, March 12, 2018, http://www.foxnews.com/us/2018/03/12/college-student-kicked-out-class-for-telling-professor-there-are-only-two-genders.html.

17 Brad Hart, "Thomas Jefferson on the Bible in Schools," American Creation, July 23, 2008, http://americancreation.blogspot.com/2008 /07/thomas-jefferson-on-bible-in-schools.html.

18 Jack Drescher, "Out of DSM: Depathologizing Homosexuality," *Behavioral Sciences (Basel)* 5, no. 4 (December 2015): 565–75.

CHAPTER 10

1 Paul Cameron, Kirk Cameron, and Kay Proctor, "Effect of Homosexuality upon Public Health and Social Order," *Psychological Reports* 64, no. 3_suppl (1989): 1167–79, available online at http:// journals.sagepub.com/doi/pdf/10.2466/pr0.1989.64.3c.1167.

2 Martin Luther King Jr., *Stride Toward Freedom: The Montgomery Story* (Boston: Beacon, 2010), 191.

CHAPTER 11

1 Attributed to Alexis de Tocqueville by Dwight D. Eisenhower in his final campaign address in Boston, Massachusetts, November 3, 1952, https://www.bartleby.com/73/829.html.

2 Geoff Redick, "Police Raid Owner's Home in Massage Parlor Investigation," ABC6, February 3, 2018, https://abc6onyourside .com/news/local/police-raid-owners-home-in-massage-parlor -investigation.

3 Mrs. E. (Elizabeth) Charles, *Chronicles of the Schönberg-Cotta Family. By the author of "The Voice of Christian Life in Song"* (London, New York, and Edinburgh: T. Nelson and Sons, 1864), 276.

ABOUT THE AUTHOR

ELIZABETH JOHNSTON, aka the Activist Mommy, is a speaker and vlogger who educates and inspires the public on the burning social and moral issues of the day that are important to families and patriots. She and her husband, Patrick, who is a medical doctor, author, and movie producer, have been pro-life ministry leaders for many years and home educate their ten beautiful children.

The growing threat to America's children and the vicious attack on religious liberty is what dynamited Elizabeth out of her comfort zone to inspire a nation of belittled conservatives and Christians to "come out of their closets" and boldly take their country back.

Elizabeth daily triggers the Left by confronting the lies of abortion, feminism, Islam, and the homosexual agenda with wit and snark as only she can, and she regularly posts viral commentary videos, which have netted more than seventy million views. As a thought leader on topics of importance to families and faith, Elizabeth has been featured on many major media outlets, such as *Fox & Friends*, the *New York Times*, TheBlaze, and Christian Broadcasting Network.

The pulse behind all her activism and cultural commentary is her love for her family and her Savior, Jesus Christ.

For More Information:
www.ActivistMommy.com

IF YOU ENJOYED THIS BOOK, WILL YOU CONSIDER SHARING THE MESSAGE WITH OTHERS?

Mention the book in a blog post or through Facebook, Twitter, Pinterest, or upload a picture through Instagram: ActivistMommyOfficial.

Recommend this book to those in your small group, book club, workplace, and classes.

Head over to Facebook.com/TheActivistMommy, "LIKE" the page, and post a comment as to what you enjoyed the most.

Tweet "I recommend reading #NotOnMyWatch by @Activist_Mommy // @worthypub"

Pick up a copy for someone you know who would be challenged and encouraged by this message.

Write a book review online.

WORTHY® PUBLISHING

Visit us at worthypublishing.com

twitter.com/worthypub

worthypub.tumblr.com

facebook.com/worthypublishing

pinterest.com/worthypub

instagram.com/worthypub

youtube.com/worthypublishing